G000043501

'*The Naked God* is a tremen[dous] book, as timely a reflectio[n] uncertain but hopeful futur[e] Kingdom. I hope it will find [...]

'*The Naked God* is a refreshing, insightful and compelling book. Vincent Strudwick draws upon his wide experience as a priest, a pastor and a teacher as he reflects upon his own faith journey, and invites us to look again at the large questions concerning God, faith, the world in which we live – and our response.'

'All of us who wrestle with the histories and complexities of our religious faith, its challenges and possibilities, know that how we speak of God, is how we think of the world. This book is an absorbing personal and literary journey into the questions we must ask of ourselves and our societies, for the sake of a more hopeful future.'

'If the mystery we call "God" is real, then it will be beyond our sight except in fugitive glimpses through thick clouds. Its greatest enemy will not be the one who says it isn't there, but the one who claims to have mapped and measured every inch of it: not atheism; religion. This was the single great insight of Herbert Kelly, the founder of the Society of the Sacred Mission. It is an insight that went deep into the soul of Vincent Strudwick, and in this brave and illuminating book he applies it rigorously to the religious situation of our time.'

Richard Holloway, writer and broadcaster, and former Primus of the Scottish Episcopal Church

'In an intriguing blend of history, autobiography and theology, Vincent Strudwick invites us to wrestle with whatever images of God we have inherited. His cultural curiosity, driven by a conviction that the institutional church is in constant danger of becoming irrelevant, invites us to peer into the corners of both Church and society where creativity is to be found. His tone is irreverent in the best possible way, and his compassion and humanity shine through the stories he tells of life in the parish and academy, always looking for places to build, as he says, bridges of hope.'

Lucy Winkett, Rector of St James's Picadilly

THE NAKED GOD

Wrestling for a Grace-ful Humanity

Vincent Strudwick
with Jane Shaw

DARTON · LONGMAN + TODD

First published in Great Britain in 2017 by
Darton, Longman and Todd Ltd
1 Spencer Court
140–142 Wandsworth High Street
London SW18 4JJ

ISBN 978-0-232-53256-2

Front cover image: *Jacob Wrestles the Angel* by Edward Knippers, author of
Violent Grace. See more of his work on his website at www.edwardknippers.com

A catalogue record for this book is available from the British Library

Thanks are due to the following for permission to quote copyright material:
Faber and Faber Ltd for 'The Rain Stick' by Seamus Heaney; 'The Journey of the Magi'
by T. S. Eliot and 'Church Going' by Philip Larkin; the Estate of John V. Taylor for
'Valentine' by John V. Taylor

Typeset by Kerrypress, St Albans
Printed and bound in Great Britain by Bell & Bain, Glasgow

For my grandchildren

Olivia, Amelia, Billy, Eliza, Freddy, Florrie and Sidney
and all their generation.

That they may wrestle, enjoy the world and discover
graceful humanity.

Contents

*Here the Wrestlers have awareness of a church on the
move and the need to seize the day.*

Foreword

Vincent Strudwick has a wide circle of friends and admirers not only in the UK but overseas. They greatly value his warm encouragement and enthusiasm as a teacher and preacher. But even those who don't know him will sense his personality coming through this book and that same affirmation of their attempts to wrestle for the truth of things. Of particular value is his personal knowledge of Herbert Kelly and his writings, a genuinely original thinker who deserves to be rediscovered in our time. One of Kelly's early hearers was the great William Temple and it is good to have him brought to the fore again, because Temple, like Vincent, was passionate in the conviction that though Christians draw their strength from elsewhere they are to be in the world for the world. Of great interest too will be Vincent's personal take on the tumultuous decades he has lived through with their challenges to belief in God and the dramatic changes in the religious landscape of Britain.

The book's concern is with those who struggle to make sense of life, in particular how this world with all its contradictions might square with a Christian understanding of God. His foundation is the way the first followers of Jesus responded to Jesus and, as a historian, he follows this focus through the developments in subsequent ages. His emphasis however is not just on what might be believed but on Christianity as a form of being, a way of life, one which enables us to live with a grace-ful humanity. Readers will find just such a grace-ful humanity in his book with its helpful insights into the history of our times, what it means to be a member of the church and what it means to be a follower of Jesus today.

Richard Harries
(Lord Harries of Pentregarth,
Bishop of Oxford 1987–2006)

Acknowledgements

'Christianity without humanism, science, or
the sceptical temper would be a sectarian
religion, not a gospel to redeem the created
world'[1]

These words of George Every, member of the Society
of the Sacred Mission (SSM) at Kelham, appear near
the conclusion of his book *Poetry and Personal
Responsibility*. It was published in 1949 six months
before I went to Kelham for preliminary studies in 1950,
when George became my tutor. It was through him that
I learned of Herbert Kelly (still alive, but bed-ridden) and
of the importance of questioning, always questioning,
in matters of religion and theology. This book is about a
'gospel to redeem the created world', and the seeds were
planted then.

Alongside was Richard Holloway, a valued friend and
inspiration at that time, and through the years; and it was
at Kelham that I began wrestling, both as a student and
then tutor.

Among the many students of that time to whom I am indebted, Barry Collins has been, and still is, a provocative thinker and pastor, of whom Kelly would have been proud.

John Moses became a friend while I was still at Kelham. At the heart of the Anglican world, he has faithfully supported me, with criticism and kindness.

Ralph Martin joined SSM in the 1950s, and seven years after I had left the community invited me, with Nina my wife and family – Rebecca (who has compiled the bibliography) Alice, and Martha (who was born in an SSM priory) – to become associates in the Society's life and work at the heart of the new city of Milton Keynes. My gratitude to Ralph for his friendship, is matched by thanksgiving for the opportunity this gave, that the whole family might have an understanding of a questioning Christianity, and be part of it in different degrees, with all its uncertainties. I am deeply grateful for this, and for them.

I have been fortunate to serve under bishop Simon Phipps (author of *God on Monday*), and then two distinguished bishops of Oxford: Patrick Rodger and Richard Harries, who (like Simon) have stimulated, understood and encouraged me. With colleague Keith Lamdin in the Oxford diocese, we were constantly engaged with the ever-changing culture of church and society, and Keith's insight and professionalism was an ever present spur.

I am grateful to the staff and students of the St Albans and Oxford Ministry course from 1988 to 1997 who had to cope with my efforts to bring an SSM curriculum and style of teaching to a non-residential course, as well as exploring links with the University.

It is to Dr Geoffrey Thomas, then Director of the Oxford University Department for Continuing Education and Founding President of Kellogg College that I owe enormous thanks for enabling me to teach in the Department and develop a style of theological education for adults that reflected the formation I had received.

Colleagues and students in both, especially Angus Hawkins, were marvellously responsive, as were members of the faculty of theology, including Henry Chadwick, John Macquarrie, John Fenton, Keith Ward, Diarmaid MacCulloch, Martyn Percy and many others.

Philip Roderick, of 'Quiet Gardens' and 'Contemplative Fire', is someone to whom I am also indebted for his exploration of spirituality with those for whom 'church' has become painful or alien.

John Morgan of the Graduate Theological Foundation (GTF) in the USA, together with members of the faculty there, and many among the network of GTF students, enabled opportunities for me to develop ideas that are explored in this book, as well as sponsoring an annual lecture on religion in public life, kindly offered and hosted by the President (Jonathan Michie) and Fellows of Kellogg College. As a constant supporter of these lectures and the project, I must mention with appreciation my colleague Michael Yudkin.

Then there are the wrestlers, whose number include Yvonne Antrobus, Susan Harrison, Ilona Keeping, Judith

Longman, Jill Pugh, Rob Ramsay, Veldes Raison, Miranda Salmon, Nina Strudwick, Doff Wheatley and Jill Wolfe. We all began in different places, and the outcome has been different for each. In the nature of wrestling, we do not necessarily agree, but we have discovered an ability to respectfully differ, while agreeing on the importance of the issue and the integrity with which other opinions are held. Thank you for your friendship, and for your share in the resulting work.

Finally my thanks are to Jane Shaw, scholar, colleague and most loyal of friends, without whom I could not have presented what began life as a seminar series. That it now appears as a book is due to her. I am very grateful.

However, I take responsibility (of course) for all the flaws and errors in style and content that you may find.

Vincent Strudwick

PRELUDE

The Wrestlers

The worship of 'Religion' has become a great
stumbling block in the way of the worship
of God
(Herbert Kelly, 1917)

Heart in Pilgrimage

It was sixty seven years ago that I first met an aged Herbert Kelly, thirty four years after he had written the statement above. For me, that statement opened a whole new way of looking at life, my experience, the world we live in, and 'God'.

I grew up in the 1939-45 war, at first in London in the Blitz going to bed each night in the Anderson shelter as the bombs fell around and playmates disappeared; then as an evacuee, and finally in a new home in Kent, where I went to school. When the war ended, I had what was then called 'Matric' (the leaving certificate if you were not going into the sixth form), but was not sure what to do, and got a job as a clerk at the War Damage Commission, compensating people who had been made homeless by the bombing. The experience of the war had left an indelible mark. How could human beings act like this? How might I be on the side of those who saw life differently? I had toyed with the idea of offering myself for ordination, but it wasn't until I met an ex-naval chaplain who told me about the Society of the Sacred Mission at Kelham, that I thought it would be possible.

Kelly had founded the Society of the Sacred Mission, a missionary brotherhood, which also trained men for ordination, and it was there that I went in 1950 to explore for the best part of a year, before I was called up for National Service and became a junior officer in the RAF Regiment, instructing young pilots of roughly my own age in the use of small arms, ground combat, and 'escape and evasion' if they were shot down in enemy territory. It was the very opposite of what I was hoping to do; but it was also my first experience of teaching, and I found I could do it, and it was very enjoyable. Returning to Kelham in 1952, I completed the ordination course, became a professed member of the Society, and was sent to study history and economic history at University before being ordained priest in 1960; the year that the Church of England became conscious (after a post-war boom) that numbers, influence and understanding of what the Gospel was all about, was declining. I began teaching on the theological course.

It was in these years at Kelham, as I shall describe later, that I came deeply under the influence of Kelly's ideas, and was particularly influenced by George Every, one of my tutors, in beginning to understand the distinction between 'God' and 'Religion', and how important it was to examine and interpret the history of the Church in its global setting, constantly changing, and always needing renewal. In a curious way Kelly and these people at Kelham were 'outsiders' to the main players in the religious history of the time; overlapping, sometimes significantly, but 'at the edge'. Unconsciously I think I have followed in that tradition.

The 1950s were days of inclusive Anglicanism, when being 'C of E' is what you were if you were English! A majority of people were christened, married and buried in Church, most of them in the Church of England, and if you had no religion at all, C of E was what you put down on any official form you were offered.

This stands as a great contrast with today. Now, a startling majority of the population in the UK and large numbers in the whole western world have become estranged from Church and what it is assumed is required of those belonging, in terms of what they believe about 'God,' Scripture and the church's 'raison d'être'. Many others of an older generation have been disappointed or angered by their experience of 'Church' and alienated from it for a variety of reasons. The recent Report of the Commission on Religion and Belief in British Public Life[1] (which I shall later refer to as the Woolf Report) describes this changing landscape. There is a startling rise in the number of people (over half the population) describing themselves as having no religious belief compared with only 12.5 per cent as late as 2001.

The decline in affiliation to the Church of England is the most significant factor in this trend, although it has been accompanied by a rise in evangelical and Pentecostal membership. Members of other faith traditions now number one in ten of the population. They have younger age profiles, and their numbers are therefore set to grow.

'Globalisation' is an umbrella term, but it is one factor in understanding the increase in the *pace* of change in British, European and American religious affiliations which the past twenty years have seen; and for a long time I considered we were at another key moment in the cyclical changes in society and the church which have occurred throughout Christian history and which I describe in a later chapter. However, this 'Age' of the church, which is seeing the transformation of global politics by climate change, war, mass migration, civil unrest, and terrorism, I now consider to be in a different category, needing radical new appraisal and action. This is the context for all our thinking about belief, God and the future of the Church at this time.

The Market State and Beyond

A significant thinker who identified a good deal of what we are experiencing and its outcomes was Philip Bobbitt with his concept of the 'Market State'. [2] Nation states have become part of a globalised world of 'market states', whose norms of justice and values are only in part the remnants of those of former faith communities. In the west, where there is an increasingly invisible Christian meta-narrative – what we might call a Christian overarching interpretation of history and values, informing behaviour – society is embracing new values maximising *choice* as the primary 'good', with an outcome of self-interest being a guiding moral principle. Self-interest of course has always been part of human nature, and in the modern period already had its evangelists, from Adam Smith onwards. More recently however, there are many others including Ayn Rand, who not only defends selfishness as a virtue, but attacks, as destructive to society, the traditional values of Christianity,[3] especially self-sacrificial love. For Christians this is the heartbeat that lies at the centre of how humanity may understand, and contribute to the way both humankind and the world in which we live may flourish.

There is now a younger generation, totally detached from 'church' and its theology and history. They are not wrestling with the nature and outcomes of change in the values 'compass' because they have no tools to wrestle with; but many are disillusioned with politics, religion and most institutions. Life is tough, and very worrying. In the Woolf report it is recorded that 'A senior figure at the BBC remarked that the British public has such a poor religious literacy that a modern audience would be baffled by the Monty Python film *Life of Brian* because it would not understand the Biblical references.' I have tested this out informally, and found it rings true.

But how much religious literacy did the very first generation of Jesus' followers have? It was patchy at best. What did *they* hear? They were frightened and confused after the crucifixion of Jesus, but began to be aware of the spirit of Jesus' self-sacrificial love bonding them, and enabling them to live 'The Jesus Way'. They rose above the fear and confusion and danger, and did so with such dedication that they attracted attention throughout the Empire. But what brings about that kind of conviction?

Towards 'Something Understood'

In terms of 'story', it is Pentecost, or 'Whitsun' as the English used to call it, celebrating the coming of the Holy Spirit that launched the disciples into the adventures and missionary activity described in the Book of the Acts of Apostles; but as we look at the history of the oral tradition and letters unfolding in what we now call 'The New Testament', we see ordinary human beings wrestling with the experience they had with Jesus, both intellectually and in deep soul searching, and in this process finding a new sense of direction, purpose and energy.

So what of today and tomorrow?

In my experience of teaching before and around the Millennium, as the pace of change quickened, the University of Oxford, both in the Faculty of Theology and in the provisions of the Department for Continuing Education, drew many people to its courses, often professing to be 'spiritual but not religious'. They have been designated the SbnR generation, and are representative of the decline of those belonging to a church. How might they be invited and encouraged to wrestle and consider what the church stands for? I needed help from that older generation, disillusioned with the institutional church in varying degrees and many having given up attending, but knowing something of the history, and wanting to scratch an 'itch' that the Gospel might have something which would nourish them that the church, in its present form, was not providing.

In 2010, while still doing a little tutorial work, I had much more free time, and I placed a notice in the local parish newsletter of the village in which I live in Buckinghamshire, inviting anyone who had left church-going and experienced a sense of loss perhaps; or who was still going, but felt frustrated or angered by the experience; or who was just curious; to join me in the Red Lion over a pint. It read like this:

Wrestling

No, not the sort we used to watch on TV, but an opportunity to tease out the joys and sorrows of what it means to be human. If anyone, over the summer, would like to spend some time wrestling with the notions of God, humanity and the church, then I'd be happy to sit in the pub for three evenings, and lead discussion on each in turn, over a pint. If you've given up on God, and the church – or come occasionally to church belonging but not believing; or if you enjoy an open discussion because you care about your children's future, you'll be welcome to join me in this conversation.

*There's no expectation of an 'out-come'; that will
be different for all of us.*

I didn't have a lonely pint. Eight people turned up,
and the following summer this developed into regular
meetings, which settled down to about a dozen people,
out of which the idea for this book emerged. In a 'seminar'
atmosphere, it took shape, and while (as I foretold in my
notice) the outcome of the seminars has been different
for all of us, the result for me is in the following pages,
shaped (I might almost say goaded) by the critical insight
and creativity of the group as a whole, to whom I am
enormously grateful.

In our twenty-first-century context, we revisited issues
I had wrestled with for over half a century. I found myself
renewing my gratitude to literally hundreds of teachers
and students, scattered across the world, whose eagerness
to engage, and whose friendship as we learned together,
had been a continuing inspiration.

Early in my Kelham years, I was arrested by the story
of Jacob. A real person? That's hard to tell for, while the
Jewish written tradition dates from the eighth or ninth
century BCE, this was a thousand years after the story
was first told. Like the rest of the Jewish Scriptures, it later
became part of the Christian Bible. 'You have wrestled
with God and with humanity, and have overcome,'
paraphrases the heart of the story in the text (Genesis
32:28). As the energetic painting by Edward Knippers
on this book cover suggests, wrestling can be a colourful
and confusing business. Yet after the wrestling, Jacob

is blessed. 'I have seen God face to face' he says, and he is re-named 'Israel', the embodiment of the emerging Jewish religion.

So for me all wrestlers are 'Jacobs', the iconic embodiment of all wrestlers embracing family, friends, colleagues, students and passing strangers on plane or train, who have and are engaged in the struggle for graceful humanity.

An Outsider[4] in Company?

In this book, we begin with God, religion and the church in history, and proceed to envision the church in a post Christian, plural society. I am examining issues, I hope seriously; but it is not a book of original ideas. I tend to agree with the late Umberto Eco that when talking about humanity, you will probably find that Aristotle had thought of it first. I do include a good deal of history, but interpreted by my own experience in the twentieth and twenty-first centuries. History is never pure; it is selected and packaged by the historian. According to R. G. Collingwood, the influential English philosopher and historian: 'St Augustine looked at history from the point of view of the early Christian; Tillemont from that of the seventeenth-century Frenchman; Gibbon from that of the eighteenth-century Englishman; Mommsen from that of a nineteenth-century German. There is no point in asking what was the *right* point of view. Each was the only one possible for the man who adopted it.'[5] History, like life as we experience it, is a babble of voices, and the wrestlers' voices are harmonised in their concerns, but not necessarily in their responses. I, as the author, take responsibility for the prelude, interlude and postlude.

The history in this book is written from the point of view of a boy whose mother was a Victorian, brought up in the world of the British Empire which then comprised one fifth of the world's population, conscious of American 'cousins', and belonging to a worldwide Anglican Communion with ecclesial links going back centuries.

History is story, and this is the only way I can tell it. We study history to understand the world we live in, the stories that lead up to our story, and to engage with who we are, and what we might become.

I am seeking to bring this historical approach to issues that have been faced in different ages of the church, extending it through the changes of my own history and life time, culminating in a time of civil conflict and global peril, with large numbers of migrant peoples on the move, a renewal of 'nationalism' fed by populist leaders, and the constant threat of radical terrorism across all borders. I am hoping that 'outsider' readers (whether of church or society – or both) may be able to locate their own life-story within the 'off centre outsider' framework of my experience, latch on to the narrative, and wrestle in faith, hope and love towards a glimpse of the mystery of God, the universe, humanity and themselves. The book is principally meant for such 'outsider' readers, not academics who may be irritated by my simplistic rendering of some scholars' complex work. The bibliography leads everyone interested to the sources.

Possible Impossibility

If you have the patience to read on, you will discover that 'God' does not mean "Im up there'; and that 'Faith, Hope, and Love' are all interpreted. Faith is not the blind expectation that 'God' will make everything all right for us, but a journey; hope is to be distinguished from the false 'optimism' that somehow everything will be all right; and love is not sentimentality. And more.

Do Christians have anything to say and do in this crisis situation which is global, still unfolding, and threatens both the sustainability of the planet, and the future of our civilisation? Like Corporal Jones in the UK sitcom *Dad's Army* I am tempted to call out 'Don't panic!' In our localities we can work for a plural society of mutual respect, to image in our corporate fellowship the 'Jesus Way' of the Apostolic Church, together with an understanding and respect for all those of other faiths in our community.

At the same time there must be an interplay with the leadership of our respective Churches, the leadership and local expressions of the other faith communities in our nation, as with Government we all seek to establish a common vision and shared understanding of the fundamental values by which we live. Out of this, the

Woolf report, cited earlier, hopes there may be a statement of the principles and values that underpin public life for the common good. Is such a hope possible of fulfillment? If we listen can we hear at least the stirrings of hope being fulfilled?

A poem by Seamus Heaney called 'The Rain Stick', is based on his experience of a drought when using a cactus stalk as a channel, he found water.

> Upend the rain stick and what happens next
> Is music that you never would have known
> To listen for
> In a cactus stalk
>
> Downpour, sluice-rush, spillage and backwash
> Come flowing through. You stand there like a pipe
> Being played by water, you shake it again lightly,
>
> And diminuendo runs through all its scales
> Like a gutter stopping trickling. And now here comes
> A sprinkle of drops out of the freshened leaves.
>
> Then subtle little wet of grass and daisies;
> Then glitter-drizzle, almost breaths of air.
> Upend the stick again.
> What happens next
>
> Is undiminished for having happened once,
> Twice, ten, a thousand times before.
> Who cares if all the music that transpires

Is the fall of grit or dry seeds through a cactus?
You are like a rich man entering heaven
Through the ear of a raindrop. Listen now again.

When you have reached the end of the book, the poem
is repeated.
Listen then again.

PART 1

In these three opening chapters, the wrestlers explore and re-frame difficult questions about God, the Bible, spirituality and the Church. Beginning with the 'naked God' of the book's title, we go on to look at the ways in which the earliest Christians emerged and their understanding of 'the Way,' how the institution of the Church developed and, in time, came to freeze its assets.

CHAPTER 1

The Naked God

'So we say that when everything (describing
God) is removed, abstracted and peeled off so
that nothing at all remains but a simple 'is,' that
is the proper characteristic of God's name.'

So wrote Meister Eckhart, a German Dominican friar
born in 1260, in his *Opus Tripartum*. For him, 'Esse est
Deus' – 'God is Being.' That for him was the Naked God,
stripped of all verbal, religious and cultural clothing.

Every generation puts 'clothes' onto God to help their
understanding; but the underlying reality of God – God as
Being – still lies behind those garments. Each generation
has to clothe God anew. If we go on clothing God only
with garments that are suitable for medieval Christendom,
or any other age, then we can hardly expect that God will
be understood in the twenty-first century.

Religion's Embarrassing Affair with Clothing God

The Christian Church in its institutions, designed to make available the mysteries of God, has, I believe, succeeded rather in locking them up. Too often, Christian faith is presented as believing the impossible in order to practise the unknowable for a goal that is a fantasy. All of my life, as both an historical theologian and a priest, I have felt myself to be in the business of 'decoding'. One of the problems for twenty-first-century people exploring Christian religion is that we have not made available to them the key to the codes. Both the concepts and language of religion, as well as its rituals, are heavily encoded by the culture in which they emerged. In order to understand what is being said, we have to do some code cracking, and then some re-clothing of God for our times, while recognising that it is *our* clothes that we are placing on God's reality.

We come to that process of re-clothing with resources; in the Christian tradition we have images and language that can arrest the attention of the future age of the church, even in its very different cultural context. That is the power of Eckhart's work: he brings to light something that is eternal, and catches our attention with it. In particular, it can often be the 'subterranean' resources that bring us to an awareness or revivification of a sense of the Divine – and that often happens *in spite of* the official histories and official language of the church. And when it does happen it can shock some in the pews.

Take, for example the publication of John Robinson's (in)famous book *Honest to God*. In 1963, I was sub-Warden of Kelham's Theological College and Tutor in Church History. The decade of the 1960s was unveiling huge changes in society, with Carnaby Street, The Beatles, Dr Who and a new sense of freedom and adventure. It was in this year that John Robinson, an Anglican New Testament scholar, wrote a little paperback book entitled *Honest to God*. As a Lecturer at Cambridge University and Fellow and Dean of Clare College, Robinson had written many academic books, but in 1959 he had moved from academia to become Bishop of Woolwich. Now, following an accident and while recovering in hospital, he wrote a popular book exploring ideas about God, the church and worship. Attempting to use non-theological language, he wrote of God as 'the ground of our Being' and Jesus as 'the man for others.' Drawing on the German biblical scholars with whom he was so familiar, he made an attempt to share the way God had become 'mythologised' in the language of the church, and by presenting what lay behind this process, he suggested that readers could think in less confined terms about the church and what it is for; about worship and its nature and purpose; and about what might be proposed as a 'new morality' arising out of this. Robinson drew on the work of the German Lutheran Dietrich Bonhoeffer (killed by the Nazis towards the end of the Second World War). In *Letters and Papers from Prison* Bonhoeffer had written of 'Religionless Christianity'. Robinson admitted he was not sure what Bonhoeffer meant by this, but I think Bonhoeffer, who had visited Kelham in March 1935, had picked this up from Father Kelly, on the basis of Kelly's distinction between God and Religion. In a letter from Tegel prison in 1944, Bonhoeffer asks 'How do we speak "secularly" about God? How can we be "religionless-secularised" Christians?'[1]

This immediately rang a bell. I was very familiar with what Kelham's founder Herbert Kelly had written in his book *The Gospel of God* that he was concerned to talk about God, not religion; and that it was important that these two things were not confused: they are not the same thing.[2] Time and again he would ask: What does God do? Does God do anything or is God just a name for our ideals? In 1963, having been formed by Kelly's distinctive questions, I felt I was on familiar ground and embraced Bonhoeffer's thinking on 'Religionless Christianity' with some excitement, thinking (unlike Robinson) that I *knew* what it meant. It was to be concerned with our experience of God in the world, on the streets, in the everyday; it was 'to be there for others.'[3] Religion with its intellectual formulations about God is necessary; but people also need pointers to the God whom they can *experience*. Over the next few years at Kelham, we hosted many gatherings of university students, youth clubs, and other groups of young people who were excited by thinking through the issues the book had raised. As in the wider world, the Society was divided. The Sub Prior wrote a hymn, which caught on, and appears in many hymnbooks today:

We find Thee Lord in others' need
We see Thee in our brothers
Through loving word, and kindly deed,
We serve the Man for Others.

Of course there were those in the community who were shocked by it and what was happening. In that sense, we were a microcosm of the church at large; but it was four years later, in 1967, that I discovered evidence of the link with Bonhoeffer. As a visiting chaplain at Dartmouth College in the USA for the best part of that year, I attended a talk by Eberhard Bethge, Bonhoeffer's former student, and later biographer. Afterwards he sought me out and spoke to me, and said that on his visit to Kelham, Bonhoeffer had attended Kelly's lectures, and that they informed his theology when he set up the seminary at Finkenvelde with its monastic pattern of community life, silence, and work in the community (very similar to the St Anselm community that Justin Welby has established at Lambeth, but in a much more dangerous context).

We are at a strange crossroads now across the generations. There are those of – approximately – middle age and above, who know the language and garments of the God of their youth and their years of growing up. They know about religion; they have questioned the sense of God that is familiar to them, and they have sometimes got cross about it; but they know the basic God language. A few of them remember John Robinson's *Honest to God*, and for some it was liberating; for others anxiety-producing. For Robinson took off God's clothes and said look: here is God! God is existence. He echoed Eckhart's words of some seven centuries earlier.

And then there are the generations below them, who know nothing (or very little) about religion, and its possibilities. In that sense the younger generations have no God to wrestle with; they have spent little if any time considering whether God's garments are any longer suitable; and they certainly cannot crack the codes. They therefore have little (if any) sense of the history of Christianity, and therefore no or few resources upon which to draw.

In presenting God to the world, then, the Church has to speak to people with very different experiences, including many for whom the past is an unknown country; and that has never before been the case in the particular way that it is now. That is why we are at a distinctive crossroads moment.

We may not all have the resources of the tradition to draw upon, but we do all have experience upon which we can be invited to reflect. I have seven grandchildren and, with more space and time in retirement, I have delighted in watching each of them as babies and then as toddlers and then as children *notice* people and things, and learn how to relate to them or use them.

What part does experience play in the ways in which we understand and practise our religion?

Experience and Contemplation

In the Christian tradition, the starting point for understanding 'Being' is not the Bible but experience; and then comes reflection on that experience and contemplation. The three Abrahamic religions, Judaism, Christianity and Islam, offer stories of *interpreted* experience in their sacred texts, which become part of the followers' reflection as they attempt to understand their own experience. Learned knowledge about the world (science broadly writ) becomes part of this reflection, and may change the followers' understanding of the story. It is a continuous and fluid process.

Eckhart encourages us to empty our minds of all concepts of God. If you have an 'idea' of God, forget it, he says. God is primarily and fundamentally just essence. This reminds us that God is beyond understanding. The un-knowableness of God is a strong theme across the religions: the great twelfth-century Jewish rabbi and philosopher Maimonides is believed to have said: 'If anyone tells me they know what God is, let him be thrown out of the synagogue.' Judaism puts questions at the very heart of its faith. Christianity has tended more towards certainties.

At the very end of the twentieth century, the Anglican theologian John Macquarrie wrote in his book, *On Being a Theologian*, 'We are not looking for an entity at all, or anything that can be conceived as an object among others.' He continues, 'We must be highly suspicious of the traditional formulation of the question of God, a formulation which runs "Does God exist?" For this question contains implicitly the idea of God as a possible existent "entity."[4] God is not an entity but Being. Macquarrie therefore suggests if God is 'Being' then we might re-formulate the question 'Does God exist?' to 'Can we regard "Being" as gracious?'

If God is Being rather than entity, that also means that we have to rethink theological activity as serious exploratory play rather than 'truth,' for we are always in search of ways of expressing the Being that is God, knowing that God is ultimately beyond our understanding. That serious exploratory play has, as its starting point, being open to God. We can choose to give hospitality to God.

It is to Etty Hillesum that we owe the wonderful phrase 'giving hospitality to God'. Hillesum (1914-43) was a young Jewish woman living in Amsterdam who began to keep a diary after the Nazi invasion of Holland; when she was taken to a local 'holding' or transit camp for Jews, she began to write letters which were later published with her diary.[5] She was part of a bohemian and intellectual coterie; she was bright, energetic, restless and always positive. She had no formal religious commitment but she was one of life's explorers. At first, Hillesum was on the Jewish Council set up by the Nazis to 'manage' the gradual displacement and extermination of the Jewish community – although at the time the Jewish community was not aware of their ultimate fate. Hillesum's awareness of the inhuman treatment of her compatriots, and gradually her friends and family, brought her to the decision to join the group *in* the camp, which led finally to her deportation and death in Auschwitz.

As Hillesum both witnessed and experienced the hatred, cruelty and brutality of her captors, she recorded her thoughts and feelings. Those who were religiously observant asked questions about the absence of God: Where was He? Why did he not intervene? It was in Auschwitz that some of them put God on trial. Hillesum, who did not believe in the 'religious' God, nevertheless began to have conversations with – what? Let's call that conversation partner God. She came to the conclusion that God is only real and visible when a human life offers God hospitality. 'When in our being we reject hatred, refuse anger, continue to forgive both ourselves and others, God is born again and is present in our compassion.'

Was this merely a conversation with herself, using the concept of God? Perhaps it was to begin with, but then she records that she 'learned to kneel,' the traditional attitude of worship for Christians, but one which she had to learn as a Jewish woman. She wrote: 'That is my most intimate gesture, more intimate even than being with a man. After all, one can't pour the whole of one's love out over a single man, can one?' This description of prayer, as both a pouring out of love and an embracing of life with love, is striking. Hillesum was exhibiting a gracious hospitality to God, and a graceful humanity.

I have told Hillesum's story because it is (for me) movingly powerful, and it comes from experience. We can find a similar call upon such experience in the traditions and doctrines of the Church, but we may find they require a bit of code-cracking.

The Communion Code

The Greek Orthodox theologian, John Zizioulas writes, 'The being of God is a relational being: without the concept of communion it would not be possible to speak of the being of God – it is communion which makes things "be": nothing exists without it, not even God.' There, in theological language, is what Hillesum said more plainly, and in a way with which we might more easily identify. Zizioulas contrasts the dogmatic theologians of the Western Church, tending to explain belief in terms of statements about God, with the Eastern Fathers, who (like Eckhart) spoke of the 'Being of God'; but they developed this by saying 'God becomes real only in communion, because it is communion that makes things "be"'. 'Nothing exists without it, not even God.' For them 'the being of God could be known only through personal relationships and personal love. Being means life, and life means communion.'[6]

In his article on 'The Holy Spirit' in the *Oxford Dictionary of the Christian Church*, Colin Gunton quotes Zizioulas as saying that the Church is not just an institution but also a *mode of being*. 'While the Son institutes the Church, it is the function of the Spirit to constitute it ever anew in the present as the body of Christ.'

The Christ of Faith is a corporate personality; 'not the one who aids us in bridging the difference between Christ and ourselves, but he is the person who actually realises in history that which we call Christ, this absolute relational entity, our Savior.' Zizioulas says 'If the Church is to be truly Apostolic, she must be historically and eschatologically oriented.'[7]

This may seem very complex, but it is simply theological code for: We must know and interpret our history, but we must also *judge* that history and evaluate it in the light of the mysterious purposes of God for his creation.

So joining (or re-joining) the Church is meant to be experiencing a different 'mode of being', nourished by the Eucharist in a community of love, where like the bread, we offer ourselves to be taken, blessed, broken and shared.

Many of us - perhaps most or even all of us - have moments of perception, when the possibility of this new 'mode of being' seems a possibility. Some do not know how to evaluate them. Some ignore them. Some try to relate them to 'God,' and sometimes with frustration for - in terms of these more chance experiences - it seems like this God reality plays hide and seek with us.

There is, of course, in Christianity (and indeed in other religions) a tradition of waiting on God, offering hospitality to God in a regular way, in order to prepare ourselves more systematically. This is often called the mystic way: the belief that knowledge of God can be gained by 'contemplation'.

The Christian Naked God

Where do the particularities of the early Christian story fit into this scheme of the Naked God? We read in the written Gospels of a Jesus who experienced God as Being and ready to be experienced at any moment. He announced 'The kingdom of heaven is here' and then he said to his followers, 'You must help them see.' Between those two verses are the sayings known as the Beatitudes, each saying beginning with the phrase 'Blessed are those…'[8] Those who are blessed are those who are aware of the reality and presence of God in the world; they become so by making sense of and responding to the variety of experiences that make up their lives; not just the happy ones, but the sad and unfairly dealt with ones as well. Through this awareness, they – we – are drawn into a relationship with God, which we will know to be real.

So Jesus was always inviting his followers and the crowds to pay attention to their experience: Consider the lilies! Look at the fields! If we do so, we open ourselves to an awareness of a reality that is not apparent on the surface. It is a way of *knowing* that is at the heart of the real meaning of faith. 'The world is charged with the grandeur of God,' wrote the nineteenth-century Jesuit and poet, Gerard Manley Hopkins, and 'The Holy Ghost over the bent world broods,' capturing the connection between experience and theology.

For theology is reflection on experience (which is something we can all do) and in reflecting on what had gone on between Jesus and them, his followers – the early Christians who followed his path and became aware of God's presence – began to understand the ongoing presence of God in their daily lives as Holy Spirit. There are many complex doctrines of the Trinity (Father, Son and Holy Spirit), developed over the centuries, that need intense de-coding, but an understanding of this three-personed God began simply enough. The early Christians, followers of Jesus, came to understand the Holy Spirit as the enabler of their ability to see and relate to every other aspect of reality, behind all of which was God as Being.

After Jesus' death, the disciples reflected on what had happened, and first of all they shared their experience, which was of their involvement in a story, and also their reflection on its meaning (theology) as they put into practice what Jesus had taught them. This is expressed clearly in the opening of the First Letter of John in the New Testament:

> We declare to you what was from the beginning, what we have heard, what we have seen with our eyes, what we have looked at and touched with our hands, concerning the word of life — this life was revealed, and we have seen it and testify to it, and declare to you the eternal life that was with the Father and was revealed to us — we declare to you what we have seen and heard so that you also may have fellowship with us; and truly our

fellowship is with the Father and with his Son Jesus Christ.

(1 John 1:1)

The whole thrust of this opening passage is that what the writer and the other Jesus followers are talking about is not an idea but an experience; and it is an experience that they were committed to sharing. That experience is interpreted by theology: so experience and theology, based on the Jesus story that those followers had been a part of, go together for Christians as their way of living life in the world. This was a dynamic recipe that changed lives, culture, religion and politics for many centuries. But if it doesn't seem like that to so many people now, then it is time to get back to experience and start up the process again. And that restarting, that recipe, is a process that has happened over and over again in Christian history, as new garments have been found for God to make sense of the experience and reality for the times. I will be discussing that in more depth in a later chapter when we look at the Church. But for the moment, let's take the example of Denys in the sixth century.

For a long time, Denys was thought to be the Denys who appears in the New Testament as Denys (or Dionysius) the Areopagite. When it was discovered that it could not have been he, his writings became known under the name of Dionysius the Pseudo (or false) Areopagite, which is a bit of a mouthful. So let us just call him Denys the Syrian.

Like many Christians at the time, Denys was conscious of the time that had been spent on constructing the Creeds, summary statements of beliefs that would guide Christians. Furthermore, he was writing at a time when the books that now constitute what we call 'the Bible' had been agreed upon (towards the end of the fourth century) but there were constant conflicts over how Jesus was to be understood, and how God and his presence can be sensibly talked about.

Denys the Syrian believed that our reality rests in our one-ness with God, and that talking about him, and speaking in analogies – that is, saying that 'God is like...' – could be distracting and misleading. He believed that we can more easily say what God is not. So our best plan is to recover the experience of one-ness with God, and we do that by purging all the distractions and misleading thoughts and doings that in our lives have smothered this sense of union.

In this crossroads moment, in which we are currently living, some of us are engaged in purging those distractions to come back to that raw experience of the Naked God. Yet others of us have the experience of one-ness with God, the Naked God, but do not have the language to put to that experience, and cannot in any way relate to the language of the Church. Yet others of us might have the experience but have not got to the point of beginning to reflect on it, and may never do so.

In the invitation to follow Jesus, in the *Imitatio Christi*, we may find the desire and purpose to live out the love that Jesus showed in his life – what is often called communion – in our daily lives. It will be our experience that initially guides us there. It is an inner compulsion to plumb the depths of consciousness. It was in Jesus and it is potentially in us. It can burst out, as it did in Jesus. Meister Eckhart calls this *'uzbruch'*. This is unlocking the code of Incarnation, the Christian word for the release of God into the everyday. It comes from within – us.

CHAPTER 2

Clothed in Flesh

The release of God into the every day

The Jesus of history and the Christ of faith

That Jesus of Nazareth, a first-century Jew, existed, and
was a charismatic leader who began a 'movement'
in Palestine, is, I believe, beyond reasonable dispute.
However, surveys in 2014 and 2015 found that four out
of ten adults in UK did *not* believe this.

A different survey in 2015 designed by sociologist
Linda Woodhead confirmed that there is another 42 per
cent describing themselves as having no religion, and
that percentage is rising with every generation; they are
the 'Nones'.[1] Three generations are lost to the church,
and a fourth is currently at school. Woodhead believes
that this is, in a significant way, the fault of the churches,
whose internal pre-occupations have become marginal
to where most people are, and the training of the clergy
inadequate for the twenty-first century; added to which,

the institution is overlaid with the complex management apparatus of a past age.

There is also an ever widening gap between the lifestyles of many in Christian (aging) congregations, and the majority in the population of which they are a part; and what is perceived to be the core message is now counter-cultural. 'Godtalk' in church, in hymns, creeds and sermons, does not correspond to the experience of anything 'Nones' think of as spiritual. Nor do a lot of the attitudes.

We may take for example attitudes towards women, and gay relationships in particular; and a built in desire to have things in church 'as they used to be'. That is all something that we must address and change; but it does mean doing some hard work on the Biblical text and early history of Christianity.

Many in Christian congregations today find it hard to grasp that the historical Jesus of the core message was not Christian, but Jewish; and to say to Nones that Jesus rose from the dead because he was 'God' compounds the credibility of the Christian message for that group. Yet this Jesus of history was given the title 'Christ' or 'Saviour' very early in the history of the movement, and while the meaning of the title is complex, reflecting the struggle of his followers to work out what they thought about him, and what their commitment meant, it became the name associated with those who followed him.

So let us go back to those beginnings.

The First Disciples: from Followers of 'the Way' to Christians

In 2005, the Jewish scholar Geza Vermes[2] summed up his understanding of Jesus like this:

> Jesus formulated a simple message for a Galilean audience, about God, the heavenly Father, the dignity of all beings as children of God, a life turned into worship by total trust, an overwhelming sense of urgency to do one's duty without delaying tactics, a sanctification of the here and now, and yes, the love of God through love of one's neighbour ... an existential relationship between man and man, and man and God.[3]

That sense of an existential relationship between human beings and God was part of the discussion in the last chapter; but there is more. What was it that turned the Jesus of history, whom Vermes describes, into the 'Christ of Faith?' For it is clear, from the tradition of the churches, and the way history turned out, that such a transformation took place.

Jesus' *death* seems to have made a different way of *life* possible for his followers, in that they discovered a new way of being human; a way – and they were known as the people of 'the Way' – in which humanity was infused by divinity. How this caught on was a slow, gradual and patchy process across the far-flung Roman Empire, but what emerged was a conviction that in Jesus there had been an '*uzbruch*,' a release of God. It was this conviction - and they were not sure exactly what it meant - that they began to explore both intellectually and in their life together in fellowship.

The people of 'the Way' also began to find that their story and lifestyle was gaining attention outside the Galilean audience where Jesus had first proclaimed his message.

In the Acts of the Apostles, an early text probably circulated before 70 CE to some of the Jesus followers, a gathering is described in which many from the 'diaspora' - Jews whose families had migrated from Palestine to different parts of the Roman Empire - gathered in Jersualem to celebrate the giving of the Law to Moses, at a festival called Shavu'ot, or 'Pentecost' in the koine Greek[4] common in the Empire. In the account of this event (Acts 2:7-11) there is a list of the places from which all these scattered Jews had come, including places that we now call Iran, Syria, Egypt, Libya, Turkey, Crete and Rome itself. It was to these gathered crowds that Peter, who had been a close follower of Jesus, spoke of him in his Galilean version of Aramaic. Their experience in listening to him may have been rather like that of southern Englanders listening to a Scot. The point is not the 'miraculous' spin put on the Pentecost event in the story in Acts, but rather that, through this event, the Galilean audience described by Vermes now was extended to an international grouping. These people travelled back to their provinces with a mixture of messages about Jesus, but with a compelling experience in their hearts and minds, which changed their thinking and lifestyle.

At about the same time as the text of Acts was circulating, when many who had been present in Jerusalem at this Pentecost were still alive, the first of the Gospels (that according to Mark) was also circulating. This is a Gospel that poses the question everyone was still asking about Jesus: 'Who is this?' The Gospel of Mark has no birth narratives or Resurrection stories, and ends (in the original version) with Jesus' body absent from the tomb, an instruction to the female disciples to go and find him in Galilee, and the disciples departing in confusion, 'for they were afraid.' (Mark 16:8)

In the period after 70 CE, when the Temple in Jerusalem was destroyed by the Roman authorities, oral and written sources, such as the early letters by Paul of Tarsus (who had not met the Jesus of history, but had been an early convert) and the texts we now know as the Gospels of Luke and Matthew, and last of all the Gospel of John, were circulated. All of these texts take account of the extraordinary transformation of the early disciples, who departed from the scene of Jesus' death in confusion, into a group who spoke of Jesus as being 'risen' and of themselves as 'risen with him', though of course, they were physically still alive. Clearly their 'risen life' did not involve 'a conjuring trick with bones'.[5]

Later, we shall examine the Scriptural accounts of Jesus' birth and resurrection in critical detail, but for the moment I wish to concentrate on the compelling evidence of changed attitudes and changed lives, which the early disciples exhibited, but which was also evident in those followers from far away who had joined them. How did this happen? The answer can only be that in committing themselves as followers of Jesus in whatever confused form, they put themselves under the authority of the *way of life* he offered, testing it out, and in that process found themselves changing.

The disciples were first called 'Christians' in Antioch, the place from which Paul began his missionary journeys, and clearly the name spread in that first century. It separated them from Romans and (in some contexts) Jews, and made them potential traitors of the Empire. They were committed to living under a new regime, very different to that of the Roman Emperor. 'Christos' in the Jewish tradition means someone anointed for the task of rescuing the people from straying from their God-given humanity. Christians were living out the 'Christos' role that Jesus had held, and which now was theirs.

The Meaning of Faith

The letter to the Hebrews (not written by Paul) was probably distributed some time between the year 80 CE and the end of the century when Christians were being sought, tortured and killed. It attempts to reconcile the deep divisions between those who wished to keep the movement Jewish, and those who saw it as something new. They attempted to do this by acknowledging the movement's roots in Judaism, and in its Scriptures, while seeing 'the Way' as fulfilling its promise for the whole of humanity. It is an important stage (of which there were to be many) in the historical development of Christianity. But the letter is also a plea to its readers to persevere in their commitment by 'faith'. What did the writer mean by faith? Certainly not believing something that your brain and experience tell you is not true. Rather, the writer said, 'Faith is the assurance of things hoped for: the putting to the proof of things not seen' (Hebrews 11:1) In other words, it is a *testing out* of Jesus' authority (his kingship as they called it then) through the experience of life in following his 'Way'. The readers of this letter were to put his teaching to the test by following it, rather as in the same way a scientist will test out a theory.

This life of faith, for individuals and those in the fellowship, involved great numbers who believed their commitment was vindicated, but it also included those for whom such a commitment was a struggle, as the Letter to the Hebrews illustrates. Faith, as expressed in this text, is not blind obedience, but a continual wrestling, with the question of who Jesus was and what authority he carried, and also with what this implied for their way of life in a volatile and dangerous world, in which they were 'counter-cultural.' Hard evidence for this view from outside New Testament studies is offered in Teresa Morgan's recent book, *Roman Faith and Christian Faith* in which she makes clear that Paul's preaching is not 'a leap of deliberately non-rational assent', but rather an exercise in trust which involves heart, mind and action.'[6] That is 'wrestling' in my vocabulary.

In this wrestling, what was emerging from one of the 'in-groups' influenced by Paul, was that 'God was *in Christ*' as he put it (2 Corinthians 5:19) and that the experience of Jesus' followers was that – whatever the term 'God' meant – they were responding to a reality, and not just to an idea. They were in receipt of what the Christian Church called by the code word 'revelation'; it was, if you like, a disclosure of 'the Naked God' in Jesus. As Henry Chadwick puts it: 'In Jesus of Nazareth, humanity is granted a self-disclosure of the Creator, and the revelation of what God intends humankind to be'[7]

We get glimpses of this wrestling in the letters and gospels, which were gathered together to form the New Testament, as well as in other material that was not included in the New Testament, such as the so-called apocryphal gospels. But the experience of the very early church seems to have been that *relationships* rather than *reasoning*, were key to both conversion and persistence, among the early followers of 'the Way'.

Doing Theology

If we think about how wrestling and following 'the Way' forged a theological path, then we might put it like this: the human person Jesus was seen as conscious of giving hospitality to God; through commitment to Jesus, all humanity could therefore be welcomed into that hospitality, image it, and share it. This is understood as *theosis* – becoming God – and it can be traced though much of the Christian tradition.[8]

It is an essential part of the Anglican tradition, and Richard Hooker, who shaped so much of the Anglican tradition and writing towards the end of the sixteenth century, put it this way:

> Sith God hath deified our nature, though not by turning it into himself, yet by making it his own *inseparable habitation*, we cannot conceive how God should without us, either exercise divine power, or receive the glory of divine praise; for we are in both, an associate of the deity.[9] [my italics]

There is an enormous amount in this to unpack from Hooker, but for the moment let us say that it is this association or 'inseparable habitation' that Jesus' followers believed was made clear to them at Pentecost, and which in the subsequent years was worked through in theological wrestling to produce a 'doctrine' or a kind of 'position paper' which imaged 'God' as a Trinity. 'God is revealed in Christ,' not just an individual (Jesus) but a corporate identity, through the 'Holy Spirit' which is the experience of communion. Paul develops this and, while in the Scriptures it is a work in progress, it is this understanding of the 'God' *in communion* that enables the church to be.

Now there is another code word to introduce here, which in the Church's tradition has had a rich and equally contentious history as the term faith, and that is 'Grace'. For the moment, I wish to bypass that controversy and offer my own definition of the word Grace, which comes from the ancient Greek word '*charis*'. 'Grace is the theoplasm received by those faithfully wrestling and imaging Christ in their lives; whether or not they recognise his presence as "gift" *or not.*'What is theoplasm? It is a useful (though not much used) word that appears in the Oxford English Dictionary, meaning 'god stuff, or the raw material out of which religious concepts are evolved.' James Murray, famed editor of the Oxford English Dictionary, was the one who enthusiastically included it in the Dictionary.[10] It is in this sense that I use the word 'gracious' as the book's title: *The Naked God: Wrestling for a Grace-ful Humanity.*

The Arts, Insight, Moral Sensitivity and different kinds of 'knowing'

The 'or not' at the end of my definition of Grace is important. In Antwerp Cathedral there is a painting by Peter Paul Rubens, 'The Descent from the Cross'. Nine figures are depicted taking Christ from the Cross: along with the faithful women are Joseph of Arimathea, who came to Jesus by night because he was too scared to be 'outed,' Nicodemus, a wrestler if ever there was one, whom Jesus told he must 'do what is true', and some workmen, who may be rather unaware of what is going on. The clue to what the painting is about is in the figures each side of the central panel of the triptych: on the left, the pregnant Mary is visiting Elizabeth, and on the right, Simeon in the Temple is holding up the infant Jesus, both panels depicting passages from the Gospel of Luke. The painter is therefore portraying 'God bearers', or we might wish to say 'Christ-bearers', and appears to include the doubters and wrestlers and even the unaware in that number.

The Roman Catholic theologian Karl Rahner has called such people 'anonymous Christians', who 'image' Christ in what they do, but may be in varying stages of ignorance or struggle about what they are imaging as they do it; but they are doing truth and revealing the glory.[11] It is basic orientation and imaging the glory that are 'salvific'; that is, being the gracious human beings of their potential. These are my wrestlers, whether formally in the church or not; for as the wise Richard Hooker said, who is in and who is out is not calculated by ecclesial boundaries and numbers. This mysterious fellowship is known only to God.

It is through the arts that we often are alerted to theological insight; but it is also through the arts that we may gain that moral sensitivity which may open us to Grace.

My friend and colleague Jane Shaw explored this in a lecture delivered at Oxford University.[12] She calls 'grace' the 'a-ha moment'; the moment of realisation when our hearts are turned, and we 'kneel'. To cultivate what she calls 'a moral imagination', she describes a process that is both a description and an analysis of what I have called 'wrestling'. She calls for an 'expansion of our communities of belonging, both in our imaginations and in the reality of our daily lives' where we express and live imaginative love for people we do not know, or whom we know very slightly. Secondly, we need to enter the 'other world' of these people, their very inner selves; or to use an old fashioned word, their 'souls'. Lastly, there is the moment when there is a change of heart, and a person acts in empathy and sympathy with 'the other' in sacrificial love. She argues that it is in the humanities and the arts that people are so often given the space to acquire and develop this moral imagination. They may remain anonymous Christians, or they may kneel, and know they have been 'graced,' even though it can be the absence of Jesus (as in Mark 13 above) that tells us that something extraordinary has happened, rather than any sense of 'presence'. Faith and hope are bound together as love is imaged.[13]

This 'knowledge' through experience and the insight thereby gained are different from, but not in opposition to, scientific knowledge. If scientific knowledge is gained by observation and experiment, the world as an 'it', we are increasingly aware that such knowledge is limited and open to new data and interpretation. Quantum mechanics has over the past hundred years raised questions about Newtonian physics and its interpretation of reality, and Stephen Hawking in his Reith lectures (2016) explored further the possible implications of black holes and dark matter, expanding the interpretation and understanding of the universes. Then, while the lectures were still being offered, Einstein's theory of 'gravitating waves', which he posited a hundred years ago, was demonstrated as astrophysicists detected evidence of what was most possibly two 'black holes' colliding, which resulted in the Big Bang of creation 13.8 billion years ago. It was a pivotal moment. The point is that there is so much more to discover, and the experiments and testing go on. So it is in theology.

Nothing in this implies that the personal knowledge of our experience and insight, in which 'the other' is experienced as a 'thou' rather than an 'it' is not as 'true' as the scientific knowledge we are continually gaining. Our 'knowledge' of God is part of an on-going experiment, in which the methodology is the same, and the knowledge gained equally true, equally partial and equally provisional.

We shall examine this process of faithful theological wrestling later in the book, but for the moment we can register it as part of the way in which the early followers of Jesus 'did theology,' recognising whatever was meant by 'God' could only be known through personal relationships and personal faith, hope, and love. Through their experience of Jesus, they had found a 'new and living way'[14] of life in the fellowship.

All of this preceded the emergence of Church, Bible, Creeds and Dogma, which we now explore in this context.

The Idea of a Christian Society in the Ages of the Church

When I arrived at Kelham in 1950, Father Kelly (the 'Old Man' as he was generally referred to) had not been outside the House for a decade, and was confined to his room; but a stream of visitors, the great and the good, continued to come and see him, and his aphorisms and comments on theology and life were part of the 'twitter' of the college. I saw him only twice: once on his ninetieth birthday, when groups of students gathered in his room for tea and cake, and the second time, immediately after his death, when again groups of students were allowed in his room, two or three at a time, to bid him adieu.

However, it was in my first term that I was assigned to George Every as my tutor in English Literature.[15] An acknowledged poet and historian, George had fallen under the old man's spell at Swanwick – the annual summer school of the Student Christian Movement – and came to Kelham as a novice and tutor, eventually taking over the Church History teaching from Father Kelly. Kelly believed that we find out what 'God' means and what he is really up to in the events of history, and historical theology was the basis of the course. That other code word 'Revelation' was also re-framed. As his friend, the great archbishop William Temple, put it: 'The typical locus of revelation is not the mind of the seer but the historical event'; and 'the principle of revelation is the coincidence of event and appreciation.'[16]

For Kelly, this meant interpreting the signs of the times, and substituting faith (as I have defined it) instead of feeling, and 'the delight of learning, beholding, enjoying, obeying ... for the mere enjoyment and possession of comfortable sentiment within one's own personality.'[17] It was through George Every as tutor, friend and then colleague in teaching history on the Kelham course, that I had my mind opened to Father Kelly, William Temple, and of course, to the thinking of George himself.

George had been taught by Christopher Dawson (1889–1970), an historian (and Roman Catholic) who focused much of his writing on the important relationship between religion and culture. In an influential essay entitled 'The Six Ages of the Church' he wrote: 'In spite of the unity and continuity of the Christian tradition, each of the successive ages of the Church's history possesses its own distinctive character, and in each of them, we can study a different facet of Christian life and culture. I reckon there are six of these ages, each lasting three or four centuries and each following a somewhat similar course. Each of them begins and ends in crisis; and all of them, except perhaps the first, pass through three stages of growth and decay.'[18] He goes on to suggest that when a new historical situation presents itself, the Church, after a period of resistance, re-engages with society to present its message in the philosophical concepts and language of that age. In the second stage, new ways of looking at God and life are crafted, and reflected in poetry and art, as well as ethical priorities. The church then flourishes again. Another period of political, economic and cultural change takes place, the Church is again challenged – and so on. Dawson sees these as 'successive campaigns in an unending war.'

Dawson's six ages are: The Apostolic Age, The Age of the Fathers, when the 'mind' of the church was in formation, the Carolingian Age, the Middle Ages, The Renaissance and Reformation, and the Enlightenment. However, he recognised that the first age of the church was different from its successors. He wrote: 'The first age of the church is unique inasmuch as it was not following an existent tradition of faith and order as all the rest have done, but creating something absolutely new.'[19] Towards the end of his life, he suggested that we might be heading towards such a revolutionary new era again.

In describing his first age, Dawson outlines the issues described so much later by Vermes, of Jesus the Jew, but also points prophetically to the lack of knowledge about origins of what he called 'Syriac Christianity', which he thought might tell us a lot about the early Christian movement as a whole, but about which the church has remained silent. This has been explored and interpreted recently by Diarmaid MacCulloch, who writes about the importance of silence in the first age of the church in shaping its character, and then speculates about possible influences and cross-fertilisation between Syriac Christianity and Buddhism, Hinduism and Islam.[20]

As the church as an institution began to take shape, and felt its way to establishing a claim to be the place where the authority of God could be found on earth, all sense of provisionality began to disappear. The Empire declined and fractured, and it emerged that Christianity would be a stabilising rather than disruptive factor, attempting to settle divisions, and it would itself become a cohesive cultural community. The Emperor Constantine embraced Christianity – largely (though not wholly) bringing to an end the years of Christianity being a persecuted religion – and encouraged this stabilising process. To help that process on the way, he called a council of the church – the Council of Nicaea in 325 – and this was followed by the Council of Ephesus in 431 and the Council of Chalcedon twenty years later. These councils established the church with creeds, dogma and ethical norms, which pushed to the margins much of its early inspirations and understandings, though Ephesus preserved the term *theotokos*, God-bearer, for Jesus' mother. A Christian society was emerging.

We can argue that succeeding ages of the church followed the pattern that Dawson described, through the next fifteen hundred years. Then the gradual secularisation of the western world, which we shall examine in a later chapter, changed the pattern.

Writing in 1942, Dawson said: 'It is obvious that modern culture is too secular and modern religion is too divided for the church to be the all embracing spiritual community that it once was … Religion has withdrawn into isolated strongholds, where it remains on the defensive, surveying the land through the narrow loopholes in the fortifications.'[21]

Both Christopher Dawson and George Every at this time saw a new age coming in which it was necessary for Christians to be much more pro-active in shaping the institutional church, in a way that recognised its history but brought the institutional church back from the margins.

As I pondered modern literature in my tutorials with George, we studied T.S. Eliot, and I noted all the copies of Eliot's work that he lent me were inscribed 'to George from Tom'; but only later realised that during the 1930s and 1940s they were great friends. Eliot often visited Kelham, where he gave a dress rehearsal of his Corpus Christi Cambridge lectures delivered in May 1939, entitled 'The Idea of a Christian Society', which we shall discuss later.

Dawson, Eliot and Every all continued to develop their thinking *as the context changed.* They were conscious that the changing scene altered the way they looked at events because in these different ages, thinkers could only see things from the political, cultural and philosophical points of view of their 'age', and different insights emerged. Some, on the basis of their experience and academic professionalism learned to 'pass over' from their own context to other contexts, putting themselves in the shoes of the people of that age; and then passing back again.[22] Such people, including Dawson, Eliot and Every among them, could offer imaginative faith journeys to be put to the test. As he passed over, in the late twentieth century, George Every wrote this poem:

Come, whom no word of ours can symbolise,
Let wiring of your word in us abide;
Light us in every dark, and make us wise.[23]

In the church through the ages, 'your word' tended to mean Scripture; but George passed back to the earlier understanding of the charismatic word – made flesh – as he looked ahead. He understood that we are called to be living words.

We will now turn from the idea of human beings as living words to what I am calling 'frozen assets': the scriptures and the traditions of the Church as they came to be settled and sometimes frozen in time, far from the experiences of ordinary people.

CHAPTER 3

Frozen Assets

The Uses and Abuses of Scripture and Tradition

'A wonderful book; but there are some very
queer things in it.'
King George V (1865-1936) on the Bible

The Church of England's *Common Worship* prayer
book directs that at the end of the scripture readings
in the Eucharist, the lector says: 'This is the Word of
the Lord'; to which the response is: 'Thanks be to God.'
On a residential weekend for the St Albans and Oxford
Ministry Course, at which he was teaching, John Fenton[1]
ended the reading: 'This *may* be the Word of the Lord.'
Eyebrows were raised; and then in his address following,
he unpacked his reasoning. I shall not try to repeat his
words, but the point was that words may become the
living word of God, when they call out from the hearers
a 'godly' or graceful response. Just because the words are

in a very old text and are part of the Bible does not mean that they necessarily invoke such a response.

From the Word as 'Embodiment' to the Word as Doctrine and Dogma

The early followers of Jesus were persuaded by the knowledge of experience, gained by becoming part of the developing history of the Jesus 'Way' movement. Those who were ready to receive the word of the Lord were receiving not a text but a living word to be made flesh in them. Roland Walls, another of my teachers at Kelham, called this 'Embodiment.'[2] Wherever the Holy Spirit is, he said, there is embodiment. That embodiment is in the actual physical existence and quality of a life as it is lived. Holy Spirit is always embodied, and this is how it is described in Acts.

However, what was happening in the world of the fourth century CE – that period of consolidation of the Church upon which we touched at the end of the last chapter – was about to bring change as 'Revelation' came to be understood no longer as God's communication of Himself in people and events, but as truth about the being of God, set out in Scripture and the tradition, which should not be challenged. The code had changed, as we shall explore in this chapter.

It was in 1963, the same year as the publication of Robinson's *Honest to God*, that Dennis Nineham published his Commentary on St Mark's Gospel, followed by *The Use and Abuse of the Bible* in 1976, which came to be landmark texts in disentangling credal statements from the process of their formation in a changing cultural context, where much of what had been thought of as 'event' was in fact persuasive preaching; and the New Testament abounded with the same mixture of material as the Old.[3]

The Hebrew Scriptures, which Christians have called the 'Old Testament', are a written version of many oral traditions within a developing Judaism, built up over centuries before the Common Era. They are a mixture of saga (mythologised history), poetry, moral teaching and philosophical exploration. There are many, and often contradictory, notions of God contained in different books, as the religious and cultural identity of the Jewish people developed. These books were collected into a single volume in 275 BCE, and translated into koine Greek, the dominant language of Jews spread across the Roman Empire. This collection, known as the 'Septuagint' became the basis for the Christian version of the Jewish Scriptures contained in the Bible. While at the time of Jesus the Septuagint was in circulation, the Jewish writings in the original Hebrew were in the Temple, and were not collected and edited until 70 CE.

The basis for the New Testament is similarly in oral tradition, with the earliest written sources dating from about twenty years after Jesus' crucifixion, with many more being written in the middle to late years of the first century, and into the second.

The 'good news' about Jesus and his message spread by word of mouth across vast tracts of the Empire, and what was heard and understood varied according to the culture, education and context in which those who received it were set.

The early followers who had not met Jesus, and those in the second and third centuries, were curious about the origins of their faith, and a whole body of written literature emerged by a variety of authors, many of whom claimed to be characters in the story. Matthew, Mark, Luke and John were so attributed, but also Thomas, Barnabas, Mary Magdalene and others. We have noted that Mark's Gospel, the earliest, was devoid of birth and resurrection narratives, which appear later; and in the (subsequently called) apocryphal gospels and epistles there was a great deal of supernatural and 'magical' content. For example, Jesus makes clay animals and brings them to life; Peter baptises a lion. These were events which in some parts of the world at that time might have been expected from such a charismatic leader.

There were also texts like the *Didache*, dated as early as some of the material included in the New Testament, and claiming to be the teaching of the apostles on baptism, the Eucharist and various points of church organisation.[4] *The Shepherd of Hermas* was another book, probably second century, calling followers to repentance. It was included, with the *Letter of Barnabas*, in the *Codex Sinaiticus* as part of the earliest text we have of the Bible, written in Greek in the fourth century CE and discovered in the nineteenth century at St Catherine's Monastery at the Sinai Peninsula, in modern day Egypt.[5]

It was at the beginning of the fourth century that Eusebius of Caesarea, a Roman historian and exegete, who in 314 became Bishop of Caesarea Maritima (a Roman city in Judea), wrote his *Ecclesiastical History*. He attempted (with both the concerns and limitations of his context and time) to place the disputes and different understandings of the story and teaching of Jesus into a timeline of *faithful* teachers and martyrs who could guarantee what was the 'true' Gospel. The conversion of the Emperor Constantine would (as he thought) establish the Kingly rule of Christ; it would result in a happy ending, with all the known world following the Jesus Way.

What followed was the attempt to gather the extraordinarily diverse local expressions of wrestling, believing and belonging into a single cultural-linguistic framework that would satisfy the intellectual cravings of the learned, and at the same time be presented in such a way that, for the mass of people, it could be woven into their daily lives. So, I believe that here we have the emergence of the Christian religion, with a Bible, creeds, doctrine and liturgy, imposed from above, to establish a religious-cultural uniformity. From the Emperor Constantine's point of view, this would establish an ordered, governable society.

In fact this marked a change in the nature of what we may now call Christianity.

What had been, in all its variety, a *verbum internum* (the internal voice of God) which followers believed to be inspiration by Holy Spirit, now became a *verbum externum* (written sacred texts) which was to mould and shape both individual followers and the world in which they lived. It was a massive change, which has dominated the nature of the church through the ages to the present day; and key ingredients in this are the Bible and the authority of bishops.

The Art of Story Telling

Before we turn to examine this massive paradigm shift in more detail, let us for a moment take an example of storytelling in scripture, and consider its purposes.

The earliest written sources about Jesus were very unsatisfying for anyone who wanted to pursue the question identified in Mark's gospel 'Who is this?' and the diaspora in particular needed to understand why Jesus was relevant for them, and even for those beyond the boundaries of the Empire. There were, for example, those of Jesus' followers who were convinced that this Way was not a stage in the development of Judaism, but a movement initiating a new understanding of God's purpose for the world. But there were many gaps in the story of Jesus. To what signs and symbols and stories might believers turn, in order to try and understand what this new Way *meant*?

Was it Haley's comet that gave rise to the story of the Magi and the star in the East?

It did appear in about 12 BCE and, in the minds of many, the appearance of a comet signalled a death. Was it therefore the death of the current regime and the inauguration of a new one proclaiming Jesus as universal emperor?

Some believe that the Magi entered the gospel story when an early preacher expounded and interpreted a text from the prophecy of Isaiah.

> Arise, shine; for your light is come, and the glory
> of the Lord has risen upon you.
> Nations shall come to your light, and kings to the
> brightness of your rising.
> They shall bring gold and frankincense and shall
> proclaim the praise of the Lord.
>
> (Isaiah 60:1, 3, 6)

There are several other speculations as to the origins of the Magi story, but the writer we call 'Matthew' was not constructing his tale on the basis of random verses, but rather on a theme that constantly recurs in the Jewish Scriptures, that there will be a new worldwide dispensation, and the story of the Magi, for which there is no historical evidence, is an imaginative way of saying that Jesus is the fulfillment of this prophecy. This is who he is.

By the middle of the second century CE the story was being developed in the *Protoevangelium* which was another of the apocryphal gospels, this one being ascribed to James, the brother of Jesus. It brings together material from Matthew and Luke together with other details that are not in either. The Magi are put on camels, and actually meet with the shepherds in front of a cave. Creative theological imagination is still at work as the tradition is filled out with minor details – it is in this text that a donkey appears for the first time. The writer seems keen to hold on to the Isaiah prophecy, but emphasising the star as the guidance vehicle, a sign from the created universe rather than the Jewish Scriptures, may indicate he is reaching out to the world beyond. Tertullian,[6] writing at about the same time, calls the Magi *fere reges* – almost kings. This may suggest they come from the pagan world in peace and, in their gifts, are returning the 'spoils,' that is authority taken from the 'true' God, and now offered to Christ the King.

The fascinating process of the development of this one mythical story, through literature, art and the liturgy, ending with the transport of the Magis' human remains to Constantinople, Milan and then Cologne, where they now lie in venerated splendour, is a task we do not need to pursue here. The purpose of this little excursion is to illustrate how the New Testament had its beginnings, and offer a little insight into how and why what is regarded as the basic Christian Gospel came to be shaped. What happened here is mirrored in the story of all the early texts and traditions.

It is perhaps the poets who capture the essence of it all, as a wrestling enquiry with question marks.[7] T.S.

Eliot ends his 'Journey of the Magi' (he had borrowed the opening lines from a sermon preached at Epiphany by the seventeenth-century bishop Lancelot Andrewes) with these lines:

> We returned to our places, these Kingdoms,
> But no longer at ease here, in the old dispensation,
> With an alien people clutching their gods.
> I should be glad of another death.

Such poetic material has always provided a store of wonderful assets to the developing movement of the Way over the centuries, for it was through story, music, poetry and liturgy, that ordinary people were to make sense of what had come to them as a rather chaotic, gap-filled but intriguing message.

Towards having Rules of Attitude, Discourse and Action

This imaginative storytelling and reliance on the ongoing inspiration of the Holy Spirit was not sufficient for the politicians and academic thinkers who were anxious to construct a cognitive ordered framework. There were Christians in high places at the court of the Emperor Constantine who began to see in this movement of the Way the possibility of a unifying force that he could employ to unite the Empire. However, its diverse nature was not helpful to this aim, and so the Emperor began to interest himself in the theological debates, which formed the basis of some of the diversity (though of course there was diversity of practice as well as diversity of belief). In the end, as we noted briefly in the previous chapter, Constantine called a worldwide (Ecumenical) Council at Nicaea in 325 CE. This was an amazing experience for people who had long been persecuted and, although they all brought their local agendas, they were over-awed by the sense that they now 'belonged' in the society that had until recently outlawed them.

Nicaea attempted to regularise difference; but it did so by setting *horoi,* or boundary markers within which debate could still take place. These are distinct from later dogmatic statements, and were a first step towards 'order'; although they did not prove lasting. A creed was formulated, a calendar was debated, and Constantine recognised that bishops had local standing and authority which could be useful in establishing order; they were allowed to own land, build churches, and administer funds for the public good.

However, bishops and others strayed beyond the *horoi* and the ensuing Councils at Constantinople (381 CE), Ephesus (431 CE) and Chalcedon (451 CE) hardened attitudes, and dogma ceased to be a reflection of experience within certain boundaries. It became a required statement of faith. The canons, or church guidelines on behaviour became legal obligations, and liturgical custom became required ceremonial; increasingly separated from the *experience* of the church. Creeds and Canons became values in themselves and, with the establishment of tradition as the required norm, Christianity as a religion, and the church as an institution, took form.

It is this institution that Dawson describes in his 'ages'. The leaders thought they were protecting their assets, and wished to freeze them against corruption. Dawson writes that even during this period:'There was a continuous process of assimilation by which the church was preparing for the reception of the classical tradition, and for the formation of a new Christian culture. As early as the second century, converts such as Justin Martyr and Athenagorus were beginning to address the cultivated public in their own language, and attempting to show that the doctrines of Christianity were in harmony with the rational ideals of ancient philosophy.'[8]

Scholars have always debated stories from the Scriptures which they found hard to reconcile with rational thought. In the third century, Origen in his *De Principiis* says that some spiritual truths may only be taught by stories, but they cannot be taken literally as reason shows that they cannot be true in that sense. (Origen was significant for articulating Christian doctrine in philosophical expositions.) The great theologian Augustine of Hippo was also one in this continuing line who wrestled in this way, as for example in his thesis *On the Literal Interpretation of Genesis* in which he discusses whether the text should be read literally or figuratively. He sees the Genesis idea of 'instant creation' contradicted by such texts as John chapter 17, which suggests God's creative activity as a continuing process.

He posits divinely implanted 'seeds' in the created order, which emerge or evolve; so the 'days' of creation are figurative.[9]

This critical reflection in the very early centuries became a continuous process as the 'ages' of the church unfolded; an ingredient in the process of decline that Dawson identifies is the attempt to 'freeze' the assets in each particular political socio-economic and cultural time frame, instead of allowing an assimilation of the emerging culture, with its discoveries and insights, to permeate the institution through legitimate theological wrestling. It is not possible here to trace the process in detail, but a pause must be made in the processions of transitions, at Dawson's fifth age, an outcome of which was the Protestant Reformation. At this moment, the cultural challenge of the Italian Renaissance, the Turkish conquest of part of Europe, the European 'discovery' of America and the opening of trade with the Far East, together with scientific advances, all contributed to a feverish debate, and with it a climate of opinion among the leaders of the church focused in the Papacy, to bolster and strengthen the tradition in which the church had flourished before these stirrings.

The Wittenberg Door: a moment of transition

During this period of rapid transition and change in the late fifteenth and early sixteenth centuries, there were subversive forces at work, not least the humanist scholars and satirists. Erasmus of Rotterdam was one, and we have from him a glimpse of possibilities beneath the surface. In 1509 he wrote *Moriae Enconium id est Stultitiae laus*, usually translated into English as *In Praise of Folly*, and published in 1511. A play on Thomas More's name (he wrote part of it in More's house), it was a laugh at the whole institutional life of society: church, academy and all institutions whether spiritual or worldly.[10] The book argues that the whole power structure blocks awareness of the spiritual world which is being frustrated by church and state alike. For Erasmus there was no comfortable home in either church or state. He was to seek his home 'a corpore peregrini,' as a wandering pilgrim, seeking the reality of God.

However it was another wrestler, an Augustinian Friar who was also an academic, a person who in his Order was considered a mover and shaker, who lit the fuse that exploded in the church and marked the moment of change. In 1517, in his capacity as a University Professor, he published notice of a forthcoming debate in the usual fashion – on the church door at Wittenberg. There were 95 theses, or propositions for debate questioning a number of current beliefs and practices. The reaction of the authorities was to close Luther down; but it was too late. It was one of those moments of transition from one age to another, and the 'Wittenberg Door' was a realisation icon that became a marker.

If Luther's action was a challenge to the way the 'tradition' had been frozen, and therefore was being misused, it was also an appeal to an authority prior to that

of Popes, Creeds, Canons and Councils: that of Scripture.
'*Sola Scriptura*', scripture alone, should give authority in
the church, said Luther, and over the next few years came
the birth of Protestantism, and a new separated mode of
being church as the institution fragmented.

What Luther meant by *Sola Scriptura* we learn from
his much later lectures on Genesis, which he unfolds as
the fragmented church evolved in ways he never could
have imagined. In the light of Augustine's work, he takes
the point that 'the Word' is to be identified with Christ
himself. As he saw it, the Word was in the beginning,
and the Word was in the naked presence of God; and
it is by this Word (and he too refers back to St John)
that all things were created. God (the naked God) does
not manifest himself in anything but his Word (Christ)
and in his works (the Creation). These can and should
in some measure be comprehended, but all other things
that belong to divinity – these are mystery. So when he
discusses the biblical text, Luther is quite happy to say,
for example, that the 'days' of creation are not what he
calls 'natural days'; in other words the *text* is not literally
the word of God.

However, Scripture regarded as a basic authority,
but open to thoughtful interpretation for the present
day, was soon (a generation later) challenged by John
Calvin, who masterminded the Protestant reforms in
Geneva and proposed the *inerrancy* of Scripture; a
very different thing, and the basis for what we now call
'Fundamentalism.' For Calvin, the church was the hidden
number of the elect, true to the inerrant word of God

in scripture, bearing witness to this word in its original purity and restoring Christianity to its original form.

A Sixteenth-Century English Exit from Europe

What we in England call 'the reformation' happened rather differently in this country. While the church on the continent of Europe was in disarray, with competing versions of dissent from the medieval order and its unity broken, over in England Henry VIII saw an opportunity to consolidate his power at home and influence abroad. Under the guidance of his first minister, Thomas Cromwell, he found a solution to his domestic problem as well. He needed an annulment of his twenty-five year marriage to Catherine of Aragon to ensure a male heir and give future stability to the Tudor dynasty; but the Pope would not grant it. Cromwell, an evangelical favouring religious change in England (which Henry did not), organised a group of scholars to offer the proposition that Henry was not merely a king but an Emperor, which meant he held his authority directly from God, and did not owe obedience to the Pope. This was enshrined in a Parliamentary Act of 1533 (the Act in Restraint of appeals), which declared that 'in divers sundry old authentic histories and chronicles it is manifestly declared and expressed that this realm of England is an Empire.' A year later, England made the King Supreme Head of the Church in his own realm.

Cromwell's success in this consolidated his growing influence, and by 1538 he had persuaded Henry to authorise an English language Bible. Attempts had been made before this, but Cromwell was persistent and the reason for his success with Henry is evident from the painting on the front of the first edition, where Henry is depicted in Imperial splendour, and we see the two estates, clerical and lay, gratefully receiving the Word of God from the hands of a benevolent Monarch – the clerical estate represented by Archbishop Thomas Cranmer, and the lay by Thomas Cromwell. From now on, the Supremacy gained its legitimacy no longer only from 'divers sundry authentic histories', but from God himself, just as in the Old Testament God gave authority to David and the Kings of Israel.

While Cromwell overreached himself in his attempts to explore closer links with his brand of Protestantism on the Continent and was executed in 1540, there was no going back on the appeal to scripture. The supremacy was dependent on it. In the same year as Cromwell's fall, a new edition of the Great Bible was issued, excluding the original 'evangelical' notes and adding a preface by Archbishop Cranmer, who warned against the evangelical tendency by ordering: 'Let us keep our bounds, and let us neither go too far on the one side, lest we return to Egypt, neither too far over the other, lest we be carried away to Babylon.'[11]

The country then went through a series of sharp and bumpy shifts in a relatively short period of time, from the Protestantism of the young Edward VI's reign (1547–53), during which time the (English language) Book of Common Prayer was brought into use, to the attempts to restore Roman Catholicism of Queen Mary (1553–8), and then to Elizabeth I's long reign in which a pragmatic settlement was established and what we might recognise as the beginnings of a broad and ever-changing Church of England was gradually brought into focus. Towards the end of Elizabeth's reign, a significant figure in the shaping of 'Anglicanism' (an invented word) emerged: Richard Hooker.

Richard Hooker (1554–1600): a Foundation Wrestler of Anglicanism

Richard Hooker was a wrestler, though his background was clearly Protestant, and at Corpus Christi College, Oxford, where he stayed until 1583, becoming a Fellow and being ordained, the evangelical influence was sustained. When Hooker arrived at Corpus he was given John Rainolds as his tutor; a man with a strong Calvinist commitment, who later became President of the college, and one of the editors of the King James Bible of 1611. Hooker's views gradually developed over the next three decades; so any judgement on 'where Hooker stood on this or that' (and many have attempted such judgements) must depend on *when* he stood there. It was about half way through the 1580s, when he was Master of the Temple Church in London, that Hooker begin to write his major work, the first four volumes of which were published in 1593.

Hooker's enormous book: Of the Laws of Ecclesiastical Polity

In the *Laws* Hooker sought to justify the Church of England's position *as a reformed church,* not along the lines that his contemporary Calvinists argued that they were reformed, but rather by building on the work of early theologians such as Clement of Alexandria, Origen, Augustine and others who said that God is Law and divinity is implicit in the natural world and the laws by which it works. Humanity is bound together by these laws. 'There is a fundamental natural law, whose seat is the bosom of God, and whose voice is the harmony of the world'[12]

Hooker allowed for wrestling in the ways in which he understood human beings to be in relationship to God. For him salvation does not depend upon a person understanding the faith perfectly, or being able to articulate it. Rather, all our comprehension is partial, and Hooker is sceptical of the capacity of formularies to express the wonderful reality of God. 'We know him not as indeed he is, neither can we know him; and our safest eloquence concerning him is our silence'[13] There is a hint here of the mystics we encountered earlier.

Our ability to know God and be his 'Associates' (as Hooker would call us) is inhibited by 'the Fall', the mythical story in Scripture of Adam and Eve in the Garden of Eden, related in the early chapters of Genesis, seeking to explain why humankind does not naturally enjoy participation in the harmony of the world. The term (or code) for this is 'Original Sin' and Hooker speaks of the 'foggy damp' of original sin that confuses humankind about its sense of direction and purpose. The 'revelation' of Scripture is both to alert us to the *mystery* of God, but also to that purpose and direction that he has revealed.

It is here that we see Hooker's theology beginning to blend with the political realities of the day, and he made a number of several key points that would shape the nature of Anglicanism over time.

First of all, against those who wished to count some 'in' and some 'out' of the Church, Hooker maintained that the church is a 'mystical fellowship' whose members are known only to God; but it is also 'militant' here on earth: a fellowship of those called to follow the way of salvation, informed by Scripture, encouraged by the tradition, and using reason both to understand natural law and to discern the meaning of Scripture. Anglicans today refer frequently to holding these three things in balance: scripture, tradition and reason, and we get this from Hooker.

Second, scripture needs to be interpreted. It tells the story of 'salvation' - that is, how humankind can become what it is created to be. But the scriptural story needs interpreting; the Bible cannot speak for itself. If we try to make it do more than 'tell the Salvation story' we destroy its credibility, and if we use it as a rule of life we get into an awful mess.

Third, Hooker believed that it was for the church to interpret scripture, and in England this was done through the authority of bishops, who were the 'glue and sodor of the public weal'; that is, they were seen to perform a crucial role in binding society together in the harmony that God wills.

Fourth, Hooker understood the diversity of the churches as another aspect of the mystery of God. Other parts of the church on earth may do things differently, but the worldwide church on earth is one in its membership of the mystical body of Christ, known only to God. Each may determine its understanding of authority. In England, he argues that authority lies in constant wrestling with the Gospel, the tradition, and a changing civil context in which we use our God given reason. We see here that the whole basis for authority in public life and personal morality was being transformed.

And fifth, if authority was understood in that way, then change was not only possible, but was required. Hooker said that as history unfolds, and we learn more of the natural world and the way it works, we pursue change. In undertaking change, there may not be certainty; but that should not impede action. You take the course where the greatest probability leads you.

Hooker had his admirers in England and elsewhere during his lifetime, but for the most part, his influence was to be felt later, and England's religion in the sixteenth century remained a puzzle both to the people in the parishes at home, and to those overseas. When Elizabeth died, and was succeeded by James (who was both James V1 of Scotland and James I of England from 1603 to 1625), the puzzle began to unravel. Under James, the questions raised in the Renaissance were revived through the creativity of poets, storytellers and dramatists. But soon there was a Civil War – in the middle of the century – and different identities of Protestantism in England fought each other. The outcome of all of that, in 1662, brought a new shape to religion in this country, a shape that was enormously influenced by Richard Hooker.

In the mid and late seventeenth century, the 'new philosophers' (scientists) were opening anew the question of the relationship between the nature of creation and the way it all works, and faith in the Christian God. While there was no smooth path, and conflicting ideas and heated debates persisted, and continued to persist through the centuries, the granting of a Royal Charter in 1662 to those engaged in such debates – producing the Royal Society – happened in no small part to an atmosphere in the church and nation which we may attribute in some part to Richard Hooker's growing reputation and popularity. Assets should not be frozen, but re-assigned to serve their purpose in understanding the 'Harmonious Dissimilitude of those ways whereby (God's) church on earth is guided from age to age'.[14] Our task is to admire the Wisdom of God shining through this beautiful variety, and play our part, open to the Spirit, in God's work. Foundational to Hooker's theology was the idea that God had made humankind in the divine image. Here is how he put it, in a quotation we encountered in an earlier chapter:

> Sith God hath deified our nature, though not by turning it to himself, yet making it his own inseparable habitation, we cannot now conceive

how God should without man, either exercise
Divine power, or receive the glory of divine praise,
for man is in both an Associate of God.[15]

What it means to have a 'deified nature', and the
consequences of that for our wrestling and how we
might envision the church in the future, will be part of
our exploration in Part 2.

INTERLUDE

In this interlude chapter, we acknowledge that being on the Way is, and always has been, a difficult journey for all wrestlers. This is my personal experience and understanding of the journey, and I necessarily turn to my story for illustration, as well as to those poets, philosophers and theologians who I have found to be useful resources on the Way.

CHAPTER 4

Open to the Spirit?

Concerning 'Embodiment'

'What does God do all day? He gives birth.'
Eckhart

Theoria[1]

In our last two chapters, we have looked at how the earliest followers of Jesus experienced life on 'the Way' and how, in subsequent ages, the institutional church often 'froze' such experiences and closed down an openness to the Spirit. Now we come to an exploration of how we might be wrestlers and seekers by remaining 'open to the Spirit' and embody that in our everyday lives.

As I have described, in wake of the Second World War, and especially in the 1960s, the western world experienced a social, cultural and theological earthquake. John Robinson with his popular theological books was making us think, and it was with excitement I responded to a student who said that Bishop John Robinson was at the Kelham Chapel door and wished to see round. I leaped at the opportunity to meet the great man who turned out to be politely reserved, but impressed by the great domed chapel, and its liturgical possibilities. The greenish bronze rood by Sergeant Jagger[2] surmounted the red brick arch, lifting the eyes into the blue mistiness of the dome. George Every had written a poem, 'The Kelham Road':

> This is a place of human sacrifice,
> And on this altar stone, young men must die.
> The Green God on the great red mountain,
> Cries his burden 'Crucify,
> Yourselves, as I am crucified...'

'It is very difficult to see the sculpture' observed Robinson, to which I responded rather piously:'But doesn't that say something about the mystery...?' He cut me short. 'Not much use creating something beautiful if you can't see it' he said, turning away...

Well, on reflection, I think we both had a point, although I felt chastened at the time; but it was years later in the1980s, that I was befriended in Oxford by his brother, Edward Robinson, who at that time was Director of the Religious Experience and Research Unit at Manchester College. Founded by Sir Alister Hardy who, while assisting in delivering a baby (a fortuitous accident), had what he could only describe as a 'religious experience' – a sense of unity with this mother, and the whole of creation; from then on he saw his life as a mystery to be expressed rather than an intellectual/materialistic cause and effect riddle to solve.[3] He became a 'wrestler' and his theory was of a 'naturally evolving attribute' of the numinous in the experience of humanity, which is often unidentified and later overwhelmed by the mundane experiences that fill everyday life. The work Edward Robinson introduced me to was his own research with people who had what he called 'an anomalous experience'. Do you make room for it, he asked, and if so, how do these two levels of experience relate?[4] 'God hath deified our nature' said Hooker. Hardy and Robinson set about testing this out.

Robinson's case studies resonated with an experience I had read about with some excitement in the late1960s. As a novice at Kelham I was introduced to the writings of the Trappist monk Thomas Merton about monasticism, and they had left me cold and feeling rather guilty, because I could not relate to what he described.[5] But now I read his new book *Conjectures of a Guilty Bystander* (1966), which was quite different and excited me, as did his later *Asian Journal* (1975). He wrote of an experience he had in 1958:

> In Louisville, at the corner of Fourth and Walnut, in the centre of the shopping district … I was suddenly overwhelmed with the realisation that I loved all these people, that they were mine and I was theirs, that we could not be alien to one another even though we were total strangers. It was like waking from a dream of separateness, of spurious self isolation in a special world.[6]

In this, and at the heart of it, is what has been described as Merton's 'vision'. It was a life changing moment when, after a dream of separateness, his eyes were opened to the reality of a world in communion. It was precisely this perception of 'communion' of which I had experienced flashes, being struck by the ordinary in a way that made it extraordinary, that rang bells. It was Alister Hardy's, and then Edward Robinson's, sense that many people have these moments, but do not quite know what to make of them or what to relate them to, that drove their work in collecting narratives of ordinary people's religious experience at the research unit in Oxford.

'These things were here; and but the beholder wanting.' wrote the poet Gerard Manley Hopkins.[7] As I began to learn, the outcome of being struck in this way falteringly opened my eyes to a different perspective, which as it happened also brought a crisis of identity, a different understanding of the church, and indeed for me a questioning of the particular form of monasticism I had embraced as it changed. This led to my departure from Kelham, although I remained in close touch with the Society, and indeed re-joined them later in Milton Keynes with my wife and family, at the invitation of Ralph Martin SSM, who pioneered a new monastic venture in the middle of the new city to which I could relate. For Ralph, Milton Keynes was Merton's Louisville, and he moved the Mother house of the Society from the countryside to be part of the loving heartbeat of the new city. This journey and his continuing prophetic ministry is described in his book, *Towards a New Day - A Monk's Story*.[8]

John Moses, in his recent book on Merton, writes that Merton himself came to see that monasticism, as it has been interpreted for a thousand years, 'had been far too committed to the established social order,' and 'neglected its prophetic and iconoclastic function in the world, settling instead for mere survival as a dignified and established institution.' He goes on to say: 'Merton found reason to be hopeful for the future of monasticism as he considered the Indian ashram of Dom Bede Griffiths, the Protestant community of Taizé, the Little Brothers, and the Brothers of the Virgin of the Poor.'[9]

Merton wanted the ancient disciplines of monasticism without the deceits offered by the 'Christendom model,' but *'it was a telling combination of conservatism and radicalism – of looking back to the heart of primitive monasticism and of looking out with searching questions to the world of his day – that he brought to the discussion'* (my italics).[10] For me, this critique was to come later, but at the time, I retained what had brought me to Kelham: the conviction that self-serving survival, at the expense of others if necessary, is not what being human is all about. So it involves exploring more deeply the sense of God's presence that some people I knew had and I had glimpsed; a sense of presence that was not from reasoning, but from the opening of an inner eye to a knowledge that in theological language is called 'Revelation'. Did *'Revelation'* and *'Grace'*, theological words that we have decoded, have a reality I could develop and communicate?

Gerard Manley Hopkins' 1877 poem 'As Kingfishers Catch Fire' captures knowledge, but we have to learn his own code of language and rhythm to penetrate it.

As kingfishers catch fire, dragonflies draw flame;
As tumbled over rim in roundy wells
Stones ring; like each tucked string tells, each hung bell's
Bow swung finds tongue to fling out broad its name;
Each mortal thing does one thing and the same:
Deals out that being indoors each one dwells;
Selves – goes itself; *myself* it speaks and spells,
Crying *What I do is me: for that I came.*

Say it out loud and perhaps capture that sense of the all-pervading presence in the differences in the natural world, as each expresses the presence; in what it is made to be and do. 'What I do is me: for that I came.'

I say no more: the just man justices;
Keeps grace; that keeps all his goings graces;
Acts in God's eye what in God's eye he is –
Christ – for Christ plays in ten thousand places,
Lovely in limbs, and lovely in eyes not his
To the Father through the features of men's faces.[11]

For it is this 'mystical turn'[12] that seems to generate the self-sacrificial love and service that has characterised martyrs and confessors and all sorts of ordinary people: artists, poets, gardeners, factory workers, farmers, cooks, clerks and lovers through the ages, and across gender of course; although we may note that some of the striking women, like Hildegard of Bingen and Julian of Norwich, were long written out of the Church's history.

Much later, in the 1990s when preparing to offer a retreat at an Anglican Benedictine House, I wrote to Dame Felicitas Corrigan[13] of Stanbrook Abbey, asking her what she thought was the essence of the Benedictine vocation. She replied that she had taken my letter to another sister and they had both responded in chorus: 'That Christ may dwell in your hearts by faith; that we being rooted and grounded in love, may be able with all the saints to comprehend what is the breadth and length and height; and to know the love of Christ which passeth knowledge, that we may be filled with the fullness of God'[14] I did not know at the time that her community treasured a historic link with Julian of Norwich, through the text of her *Revelations of Divine Love*, with which her comment to me is so much in tune. Both in Julian's own century, and in every century as well as today, the structures, images and teaching of the Church did not and do not communicate a God of love in any sense that people can always recognise. So the idea seems revolutionary.

From Theoria to Theory

In this desire to explore the mystical turn I knew I was in company. Today there is a groundswell of explorers, and the German secular sociologist Jurgen Habermas, in his book *An Awareness of What is Missing* puts his finger on the reason why. He argues that secular philosophy cannot arouse in people a solidarity with all humanity, motivate people for the common good, or even give under-girding reasons why a people should feel loyalty to a political community.[15] He wishes to engage in dialogue with faith communities in what he now terms the 'post secular' society of the twenty-first century, to discover more. In particular he believes that the presence of the Judeo-Christian ethic of love has a legacy and a presence in which those of these traditions now have the opportunity to offer more about the 'knowledge' that appears to inspire this missing grace.

Back in my Kelham days, George Every had introduced me to the 'Epiphany Philosophers', a group of which he was a member, founded by Richard Braithwaite, Margaret Masterman and Dorothy Emmet, who freely ranged over the nature of humanity, religious experience, and religious language. They would go off for a week or so to 'The Mill' (I never discovered where it was) to 'group'; but the Braithwaites and Dorothy Emmet often also came to Kelham towards the end of the 1960s.[16] One of the questions posed in my presence was: Is there a way of describing religious experience in a form that can be taken seriously by those who are not believers? At the time I was doing a lot of work with young people, and it was Dorothy Emmet, with the young in mind, who encouraged me to write an article for the SSM Magazine on grace, prayer, and worldly holiness.

I asked George Every if he would write a poem to evoke my theme. I received a curt reply, which I took to be a refusal, but nevertheless a few days later he responded with this:

> Time, times, and half a time
> The cards are dealt, but the hand
> Is never right, nor enough
> Money in the wallet.
> On the outside of the cup
> Reflection transforms fortune
> Into a new tune within.

The last line became the title of the article, and for me imaged Holy Spirit as the conductor of an orchestra (or 'lead' in a pop group) who brings into harmony all the bits of my existence, creating a rhythm of life-giving energy within, and a life-changing new tune ringing out in the activities of daily life.[17]

Bonhoeffer, in a paper from the Tegel prison in Berlin, drafted an outline of a short book (to which I have already referred) which included the following passage: 'Our relationship to God is not a religious relationship to a Supreme Being, absolute in power and goodness, which is a spurious conception of transcendence; but a new life for others, *through participation in the Being of God*'[18] (my italics). The negative part of this statement relates to what I learned later from John Macquarrie (Supreme Beings are out); while the second part of the statement needs an exploration of Revelation and Grace. In his

Letters and Papers from Prison Bonhoeffer says we have to strip off the garments of Christianity – strip it bare, so we have the Naked God; and it is to that Naked God we pray, or rather who prays in us; for prayer is opening ourselves to the Presence. What this means, I think, is getting rid of the idea that prayer is asking a Supreme Being to do things on our behalf, and replacing it with a conductor who (if we allow Him) empowers us to do things on His behalf. Issuing from this is what Bonhoeffer calls 'righteous action'. And it is never too late.

In Shakespeare's play *The Tempest*, the evil genius on the island where the main characters have been wrecked is perhaps representative of the 'natural' world, who learns at the end of the play that his case is not hopeless, and cries: 'Henceforth, I'll seek for Grace!' Is Shakespeare suggesting that in humanity a recovery of innocence is necessary, and Grace which is present naturally, but is blocked out by the chaos of life in the world, is there waiting for everyone who seeks it? 'Evil' is not to be predicated to a few pre-destined Calibans, but as Prospero realises at length, it comes from blocking out Grace. So, even in the most seemingly hopeless cases, Grace is available, and may be sought.

Seeking for Grace: focusing awareness

In his book *Seven Brief Lessons on Physics*, Carlo Rovelli offers what he calls 'a scientific picture of the world' and writes: 'We (humans) are an integral part of nature;

we are nature, in one of its innumerable and infinitely variable expressions.'[19]

Each item in the Universe (including ourselves) is an utterance of the word of God in a particular and unique way.

We observe this compatibility with the natural world in children, who are curious about everything. Turn a stone, and find a slug. What is that all about? As a London child evacuated to Devon in the Second World War, I was present on a farm at lambing time, when one was brought into the farmhouse and fed with a bottle by the open fire. That opened up all sorts of questions that I had not asked before. Much later in the mid-1960s, travelling by train across the veldt from Johannesburg to Bloemfontein, there was a re-awakening of the experience, as there was flying over the great lakes in North America. These were and are just glimpses, re-awakened, and a reminder that there is something missing in the everyday: re-awakenings; but even for someone on the 'inside', difficult to maintain.[20] It is this that some scholars identify as the point of Jesus' comment in Matthew's Gospel when he says that unless you become as little children, you cannot enter the Kingdom. The sense of being attuned to the natural world, curious, alert, observant, and aware, is something that needs to be nourished, identified and developed; and re-awakened. Edward Robinson, in his research on religious experience, published numerous experiences of childhood recollections of those he interviewed, half forgotten perhaps, unidentified, but which resonated with what he could identify as an awareness of the numinous, still there in humanity, but blocked by the 'chaos' of noise, busy-ness, activity and adult expectations of life in successive cultures.

How then may Grace be sought by those who (unlike the agnostic Etty Hillesum and the monastic Thomas Merton) are not overwhelmed by it as they, and the disciples were, by a Pentecost experience – participating in the Being of God? Or how may the wrestling be renewed in those who have been met by what the sociologist Max Weber called 'the routinisation of charisma'?'

In Silence

'God's voice' said Father Kelly in the Society of the Sacred Mission (SSM) Principles 'speaks most often in the silence.' Reaching out to those estranged from 'church,' Philip Roderick, founder of the dispersed community 'Contemplative Fire', had the idea in 1992 of beginning a network of 'Quiet Gardens' in which people fortunate to have beautiful plots, small or large, would open them on certain days for people to come and be quiet. It swiftly grew as an ecumenical and international movement, allowing people who felt their lives were cluttered to be still. In 2017, it celebrates its twenty-fifth anniversary of fulfilling that need.

In the rural parish in which I live, a particular incident of the death of a Muslim child, Alan, when a boat capsized, caught the headlines in 2015, and the plight of refugees in Europe disturbed the whole community. What could a parish church do? After debate, the church doors were opened in a silent three-hour vigil to which the whole village community was invited. The church was silent; people could come and go as they pleased. They could light a candle – or not. They could leave a donation for a refugee charity – or not. Several people came who had never been inside the church; for one of them it provoked an astonished admission (to a fellow dog walker days later) that he felt he 'belonged' in this silent building, with its silent people; a public building where serious things were part of the agenda, but no conformity to 'normal' ecclesial expectations was required. He was alone, but did not feel lonely there, for he was in (silent) company.

In Company

Let us recall the theologian of communion, John Zizioulas: 'The Being of God is a relational being: without the concept of communion, it would not be possible to speak of the being of God. It is *communion* that makes things 'be'; nothing exists without it, not even God.'[21]

People explore their identity in many ways. The football team, the sports club, the pub, the Women's Institute, a shared project: all bring together people who are very different, but their difference is subsumed by their collective rapport. It happens too in many informal ways, as for example in the pub. Supremely it should happen in church. When a congregation gathers for Eucharist and other services, including weddings, funerals and baptisms, which often bring in the 'unchurched', there is the possibility for an extraordinary interplay to be brought into focus, and renewed. With all its ambiguities something of this is caught by the agnostic poet Philip Larkin in the last stanza of his moving poem 'Church Going.'

> A serious house on serious earth it is
> In whose blent air, all our compulsions meet,
> Are recognised, and robed as destinies,
> And that much never can be obsolete,
> Since man will be for ever surprising
> A hunger in himself to be more serious
> And gravitating with it to this ground,
> Which once he heard was proper to grow wise in,
> If only that so many dead lie round.

In spite of the decline in young people getting married, having children baptised or having a funeral in church, there are many (including those who are SbnRs) who still do so, having surprised a hunger in themselves to be more serious, and wishing in this public place to build on the revelation that they love each other, are part of each other, and pledge themselves to pursue this with the help of family friends and community. They do so, however incoherently, in faith that they are on a journey, in hope, that in spite of failings they can start again, and in love, which, as outlined by Paul (traveller and Roman citizen) in 1 Corinthians 13, is the divine basis of all relationships.

While on the subject of 'journeying' it is perhaps
worth noting that an amazing number of people (again
many SbnRs) now are drawn to enjoy pilgrimages, where
walking and living in company on an ancient route
brings them to a destination which they have heard it
'was proper to grow wise in'. From the famous Santiago
de Compostela destination across Europe to Spain and
the Canterbury Pilgrimage route in the UK, many less
travelled pilgrim routes are being explored and travelled
again, not so much by the pious as by wrestlers of all
sorts who have surprised a hunger in themselves to be
more serious.[22]

By Digging Deep to Plumb the Mystery of God's Presence in the World

Etty Hillesum, remember, discovered a religious rhythm,
inspired not by church, synagogue or dogma, but by the
circumstances in which she found herself. It began as a
serious dialogue 'with what is deepest inside me, which
for the sake of convenience, I call "God".' In this state she
developed her own liturgy. 'As I walk the streets (of the
Nazi occupation) I am forced to think a great deal about
your world. Think is not really the right word; it is more
an attempt to plumb the mystery with a new sense.' She
addresses 'God' in her liturgy: 'I shall always labour for
you, and remain faithful to you, and I shall never drive you
from my presence.'[23] It was when walking the dangerous
streets of her time and country that Etty was forced to

think about God's world; and in the angry world in which we find ourselves today, where the stranger is targeted by abuse or the loved one senselessly murdered, it may the same for some of us.

But it is in walking the more peaceful footpaths of the countryside that others have been, and are, forced to do the same. Gerard Manley Hopkins spoke to both when he wrote in his poem 'God's Grandeur':

> The world is charged with the grandeur of God,
> It will flame out, like shining from shook foil.
> It gathers to a greatness like the ooze of oil
> Crushed. Why do men then now not reck his rod?
> Generations have trod, have trod, have trod
> And all is seared with trade; bleared, smeared with toil;
> And wears man's smudge, and shares man's smell; the soil
> Is bare now, nor can feet feel, being shod.

But he assures us, '*Nature* is never spent' because the Holy Spirit is lurking in the darkness to surprise us with promptings.

Similar prompting to plumb the depths of the mystery comes from musicians and artists of all kinds. It was not until the Tate Gallery exhibition of his works in 2006 that I came across Kandinsky. He published his *Concerning the Spiritual in Art* in 1912 after a lengthy gestation period, and it was part of a 'mystical turn' at the beginning of the twentieth century. It was widely manifested, often in eccentric ways, from within, on the edge of, or completely outside organised religion. Writing of Cezanne, Kandinsky says that this artist was endowed with the gift of divining the inner life in everything. His colour and form are alike suitable to spiritual harmony, which captures the mystery. Ivon Hitchens, an artist speaking of his landscapes said: 'a picture is compounded of three parts; one part the artist, one part nature, and one part the work itself which has a life of its own. All three should sing together.'[24] It forms a new tune again, which expresses the artist's identity and compulsion to express it. He might have added that there is also the role of the beholder, who also sings in a personal appraisal and appreciation of what is being offered.

In this 'theoria', artists are drawing together as part of the experiment. Kandinsky writes: 'Sienkiewicz, in one of his novels, compares the spiritual life to swimming; for the man who does not strive tirelessly, who does not strive against sinking, will mentally and morally go under.'[25] I think this is Kandinsky's version of wrestling.

In summary, the quest is one in which the seeker (or even those who are not consciously seeking, but find themselves sought, like C. S. Lewis) are offered a variety of openings. What happens is always different, always personal, but whether convicted by certainty or not, such seekers may be aware of an inner presence, albeit falteringly, which has an outcome in a moral necessity *to be* the presence of God for others; still a mystery, still with an inadequate language, but part of an embodiment that acts as a sign which arrests attention. Scientists create myths, and then test them out to see if they are backed up by evidence, or not. Those who become part of the spiritual quest similarly believe they are on the 'inside' of an experiment, testing out a vision.

During the 1980s I became friends with John and Peggy Taylor, and celebrated the Eucharist (in the chapel of the All Saints Sisters in Oxford) on the occasion of their fiftieth wedding anniversary.[26] John introduced me to this poem by him. It is entitled: 'Valentine', and is a love poem that explores the complexity of the journey inwards.

> To say I love you is like saying 'God'.
> In Eden once I knew what both terms meant;
> Each was distinct, known or becoming known,
> Until, beyond the Image, I faced the Other
> And knew not how to love that counter-self
> In you or him, which might reject, or smother;
> And above all I feared my nakedness,
> Yet still my heart is yours, yes more than his,
> And his 'where art thou?' echoes only mine
> Calling for you among the tangled trees.
>
> 'God' is my dread, my hunger and my hope
> Thrown on the luminous screen of the outer dark
> While, hidden at the inmost core of me,
> He who is not I, waits my coming home.
> You too, dear love, draw me to that labyrinth:
> While needing most your separate otherness,
> I cannot reach you till I find my self.
> The more I pick these ravelled threads apart

The more they fray. Forgive me patient heart,
That I bring nought today but a lover's knot.

Taylor came to hold the view that the *only* power that
God possesses is the power of love, and regarded this
as the central truth of Christianity, which has been kept
submerged for over 2000 years. That conviction is there
in this poem, and it is there in his book about the Holy
Spirit *The Go-Between God* in which the reality of God is
powerfully proclaimed in language, symbols, liturgy and
actions. Taylor's God, while stripped of traditional clothes,
is not a non-theological God. For Taylor this God is real;
as weak as water, but as irresistible as a river. As Taylor
puts it: 'Out of those depths of undifferentiated chaos
all the multitudinous forms of existence are going to be
beckoned into being by call and response. But in that
timeless moment nothing is present except the ardent,
cherishing love, the irresistible will for communion, of
the Go-Between Spirit.'[27]

This God can be found in the universal experiences of
being human, and in a Church that embodies the Mystery
in its praxis, that is expressing the presence in its activity,
proclaiming the Kingdom.[28] I think one of the earliest
forms of the creed included the phrase: 'I believe in the
Holy Spirit, the Church...' This is a ministry of presence,
and becoming part of a Church with this understanding,
with a rhythm of worship and praxis in its common life,
may be the place of core identity in which the inner eye
of love is opened.

PART 2

In this second part of the book, we explore – from the wrestlers' perspective – the larger picture of global peril and disillusion with organised religion and the historic reasons for it. This involves history of various sorts to see how we got to where we are, as well as some personal reflections on this history. Chapter 5 engages with the history of 'living memory' – drawing on the important work of early twentieth-century theologians such as William Temple. Chapter 6, on the Church of England and Anglican Communion in the past few decades, is not a comprehensive history, but rather my own perspective and position as an insider-outsider, drawing on incidents and experiences of which I have first-hand knowledge. I hope, in speaking personally, I track this wrestler's journey *within* the Church, recognising that other wrestlers will have had different reactions to this course of events.

We do all of this history to move to the 'possible impossibility' of initiatives from religious institutions, and to recognise and encourage a movement towards an international understanding of the common good, which we explore through the lens of globalisation (Chapter 7) and the contemporary Church (Chapter 8).

CHAPTER 5

The End of an Era

Attempting to Grasp the Nettle

'The Kingdom of Heaven is at hand'
Matthew 10:7

'Like a mighty tortoise
Moves the church of God.
Brothers we are treading
Where we've always trod.'
(Student verse to the hymn 'The Church's One
Foundation')

In this chapter, we think about interpreting the tradition and interpreting the world, and so we turn again to some history – this time to the more immediate past to see what has shaped us in our living memory, and what might turn out to be our resources for the future. This 'living memory' history for people of my generation ranges from the mid-nineteenth century to the present day, in the sense that we have been able to converse with people whose memories reach back to the mid-Victorian period, and to some extent through them have been able to glimpse a different perspective as we reflected on earlier pages of written history, and tried to interpret what happened and where we are now.

As the twenty-first century dawned, an evolving 'market state' culture still had remnants of cohesion, and the Christian religion was a recognisable thread running through it. Against the background of the wars in the Middle East, and subsequent much wider political chaos, the world seemed to be running out of control. The Anglican churches, internationally, were divided over questions of authority, the way to read scripture, sexual ethics, and how to be church; and these questions and divisions continued to be addressed at an agonisingly slow pace. There was a sense that a growing number of the population in the UK was not interested in anything to do with 'God' or Church; and the Church of England's claim to be 'the Church of the Nation' increasingly rang hollow. Nevertheless things felt 'normal' enough for most church members to think we could carry on as before, while others of us saw a trend in the recent past that was threatening to complacency, and detected the end of one of Dawson's eras. We found ourselves asking: 'How did we get here'?

How did we get here?

Early in the twentieth century, Thomas Hardy wrote a poem in which he imagined himself attending God's funeral. It includes the lines:

> O man-projected Figure, of late
> Imaged as we, thy knell who shall survive?
> Whence came it we were tempted to create
> One whom we can no longer keep alive?
>
> Framing him jealous, fierce, at first
> We gave him justice as the ages rolled,
> Will to bless those by circumstance accurst,
> And longsuffering, and mercies manifold.
>
> And tricked by our own early dream
> And need of solace, we grew self-deceived,
> Our making soon our maker did we deem,
> And what we had imagined, we believed.

The poem was written between 1908 and 1910, around the same time that Herbert Kelly, now with his embryonic Society and students at Kelham, wrote *An Idea in the Working* (1908) and an Anglican priest named J. N. Figgis (who had been Rector of Marnhull in Dorset, made famous by Thomas Hardy as 'Marlott' the home of Tess of the d'Urbervilles) wrote *The Gospel and Human Needs* (delivered as the Hulsean lectures in Cambridge in the academic year 1908–9). In 1896 Figgis had joined the Community of the Resurrection at Mirfield, a second male Religious Community in the Church of England that hosted a theological seminary. (My own community, SSM, lodged at Mirfield during part of the 1914–18 war, when Kelham was requisitioned by the army.) During this time Figgis began to develop ideas about the shape of the new society that was rather incoherently emerging in the UK's cities, towns and countryside. We shall discuss Figgis' importance a little later.

On the surface much looked the same in this decade before the First World War, but the veneer of church-based national pageantry, and formal religion in the parish church, could not disguise the reality that the influence of religion in public life, and its place in the culture of English society, was diminishing. In the latter half of the nineteenth century, while there was still a majority of Christian believers, there were many who belonged but did not believe, and a growing variety of secular dissenters. However, wrestlers were at work.

In 1859, Charles Darwin had published his *On the Origin of Species by Means of Natural Selection*, a book that was to have a far-reaching impact on religious belief. Amongst those who immediately grasped the import of Darwin's theory of evolution, there were those who vehemently opposed his work and wished to retain the status quo, and then there were those who were willing to risk embracing change. Famous for his attack on Darwin was the Bishop of Oxford (Soapy Sam) Wilberforce, in a much-publicised debate in Oxford. Amongst those who were willing to take up the challenge of new ideas was a group of Oxford dons, scholars and churchmen, who embraced change, taking seriously the scientific, literary and historical material now available and publishing their responses in a book titled *Essays and Reviews* (1860).[1] However, their audience was limited to a small academic and clerical circle, and they were attacked and side-lined by the gate-keepers against change, who were powerful within Society and the Church.

Anthony Trollope provides a textured social background to this in his Barchester novels in which the institutional turmoil is movingly described. In *The Warden* (1855) we have John Bold, the reformer, Archdeacon Grantly, the conservative, and Warden Harding, the lovable man in the middle, who, with his worn out working men at the 'Hospital,' comes out of it all the worst off, in the clash between vested interest and reform. Social reform was slow to come, and in the country at large the numbers of those abandoning Christianity increased.

Attempts to Turn the Tide: Subsidiarity[2]

As the new century dawned, the position of those who embraced change had become more assured. Well to the edge of the mainstream was J.N. Figgis, developing his ideas of the 'Plural State'. Figgis believed that while the 'State' still looks on its members as individuals, people gained an identity by 'belonging' at a more local level. It is in family, Church, Trades Union, Friendly Society, Boys' Club and the Scouting movement, that people get their sense of belonging, and it is here that the corporate structure of the democratic State needs to be formed, responding to the insights, needs and traditions of these communities, as it legislates for the whole.[3] It is this part of Figgis's thinking that, I believe, has lasting value, and in his time it had enormous implications for the National Church. It was he who coined the term 'community of communities' to describe the State as it changed before and during the Great War, a term picked up and used by Jonathan Sacks (when he was Chief Rabbi) in the 1990s.

The outcome of much social thinking at the end of the Victorian era and during the Edwardian era was that in a growingly diverse and better-educated society, there was already a response in the direction Figgis urged. The development of local government was a prime devolution of power, and another example was the re-structuring of the British Army. In 1881, the army too was localised: the regiments were now the East Suffolks, the Beds and Bucks Yeomanry, the Norfolk Regiment, the Lincolnshire Regiment, the City of London Regiment, and so on. You were recruited with your mates, you fought with your mates, and many (as it turned out) died with their mates.

God, Faith and Scripture

By the early twentieth century, the wrestlers were coming into positions of power, while in other parts this 'wrestling' was encountering resistance. In Britain, the Church of England was moving forward not by addressing its structures, but by wrestling with its theology. One of the contributors to *Essays and Reviews*, Frederick Temple, had become Archbishop of Canterbury in 1896. Twelve years earlier he had delivered the Bampton Lectures at Oxford University, developing his thesis on '*The Relation between Religion and Science*' and now (in 1896), only thirty-seven years after the publication of Darwin's theory of evolution, which had caused so much controversy in the churches, there were no religious objections when Frederick Temple was nominated for the top job in the Church of England. Both in the academic community and the clergy, evolution was beginning to be accepted. However the arguments for thinking new thoughts about God, the Scriptures, the meaning of faith, and what the church is for, were complex, and those who sensed a new age were still confined to a small elite. The new theological position had not touched the population at large. That was a project still to be recognised and acted on. In 1909 Frederick's son, William, was ordained and soon thereafter appointed headmaster of Repton School, and he was one of those in the Church who would bring the new insights of theology to the broader population.

The other theologian who was to have such an impact on popular understandings of Christianity was William Temple's near contemporary C. S. (Jack) Lewis, of whom more later. He was born in 1898, the year before my mother was born. The relevance of this is to illustrate that by the end of the nineteenth century, people could have very different upbringings with regard to faith – or lack thereof: while my mother was growing up in a Suffolk village and was nurtured in the Christian faith within her family and the village community, a faith that sustained and challenged her for 85 years, Jack Lewis in his early years had quite a different experience. He perceived his father as valuing churchgoing as an aesthetic national tradition, while his atheist schoolmaster took him into Hardy's world. He wrote, as a younger man, that all mythologies spring into being to explain certain phenomena by which primitive man was terrified, and he declared himself content to live without believing in a bogey who was prepared to torture him for ever if he should fail in coming up to what he described as an almost impossible ideal. Later he was to have a change of mind and heart.

And then there were the resisters of change, who tried to turn the tide by drawing up their own new lines of engagement. Across the Atlantic, between 1910 and 1915, a series of pamphlets was published in the USA called The Fundamentals, which were devised by 'gatekeepers' to freeze the assets of the church and resist change. They were not sophisticated, but they were clear, and in terms of the 'ages of the church', they were 'counter change' but they were presented as defending a historic understanding of Scripture as well as American culture, and in doing this they had great appeal. The Fundamentals included the following:

The authority of the plain word of scripture is paramount and cannot be changed.

The birth of Jesus was a miracle birth by the Virgin Mary.

In dying on the cross, Jesus was a 'substitute' for every human being who sinned. ('He died that we might be forgiven; he died to make us good.')

Jesus rose bodily from the tomb.

Jesus is God in human form.

In various forms, Fundamentalism now began to flourish round this simple formula, in the USA, the United Kingdom and its Empire, and the western world. It found a partner in other world religions who adopted a fundamentalist stance.

The World as the Choice Place of God's Love: Kingdom Theology

When I was first at Kelham in 1950 there was the Steward's Office, a mini shop, where we queued for daily necessities. Stuck on the wall was an old photograph of two men on a greasy pole whacking each other with pillows. One was Herbert Kelly in habit and the other was William Temple in clerical dress, as he was a deacon at the time. It was captioned 'Baslow 1908' and was a gathering of the Student Christian Movement (SCM).[4] This photograph marked the beginning of Kelly's influence on Temple. It was also the year when Temple became President of the Workers' Educational Association (WEA), a post he held until 1924, giving a Presidential

Address each year, writing for their journal *The Highway*, and promoting and resourcing all continuing education, including University Extension classes.

For Temple, the key to Christianity was the Incarnation – another code word, this one meaning 'God made flesh', which for Christians is Jesus. The 'Word' of God is not in the pages of a book, but is a living word when made flesh. In what is rather old fashioned language now, he saw the Incarnation as the culmination of the process of creation. 'God so loved the world that he gave his only begotten Son' as it says in the Gospel of John. The world is the chosen place of God's love, the nature of that love is disclosed by Christ in his life and death, and through the Spirit the eyes of everyone may be opened so that they may be that love in their every day life. This is the Gospel of the Kingdom.[5]

William Temple took from Kelly that in not spreading this Gospel of the Kingdom, the Church was failing. Kelly had written: 'The worship of the parish church is the key which should unlock the mystery of God in the world. Just so. Is it being used to unlock the mystery? Is it not being very generally used to lock the mystery up, to lock itself up, safely within the Church itself?'[6] And again: 'Football clubs are (seen) as a means of keeping young men together. You ought to be interested in the discussions of your working men, because they will then be interested in what you have to say and come to church. It all ends in that.' Wrong says Kelly, catching the reader out. 'You should be interested in the labour question *because God is*.'[7]

What Kelly was driving at, and Temple was developing, was Kingdom theology rather than church theology. Church and church services had become substitutes for the Kingdom. 'Kingdom now' is the transformation of society; while 'Kingdom spotting' is the Church discerning what God is up to in the world, and trying to collaborate with Him in effecting it. As Temple liked to say: he believed in the Holy Catholic Church and sincerely hoped that one day it would come into being.

In developing his Kingdom theology, Temple was always seeking to put God at the centre of how we might organise our lives (and therefore society) and challenged the self-interest lobby as, for example, in his definition of original sin.

When we open our eyes as babies, we see the world stretching out around us, we are in the middle of it; all proportions and perspectives in what we see are determined by the relation – distance height and so forth – of the various visible objects to ourselves. This will remain true of our bodily vision as long as we live. I am the centre of the world I see, where the horizon is depends on where I stand. Now just the same thing is true at first of our mental and spiritual vision. Some things hurt us, we hope they will not happen again; we call them bad. Some things please us, we hope they will happen again; we call them good.

Our standard of value is the way things affect
ourselves. So each of us takes his place in the
centre of his own world. But I am not the centre
of the world, or the standard reference as between
good and bad; I am not, and God is. In other words
from the beginning, I put myself in God's place.
This is my original sin.[8]

This was in stark contrast with the Atonement theology of
the contemporaneous Fundamentalists, and contributed
to his inclusive Kingdom theology. He wrote:

The Kingdom cannot come in all its perfection
for at least two reasons. First it is a fellowship
of all generations; secondly, every child that is
born, being a nucleus of that Original Sin which
is self-centredness, disturbs such degree of
approximation as has been reached. Consequently
here the figure of the Kingdom is the Cross, for
in this world, it is always winning its triumph by
sacrifice; but the Cross is the symbol, not of failure
but of triumph – a triumph to be made perfect in
God's chosen time.[9]

Kingdom Theology in a Changing Society

Temple was highly committed to the WEA and the
reason for his commitment is spelt out in the phrase

'the development of the personality'. Everyone should have the opportunity to develop their personality, not to enable them to fit more easily into society as it is; but to equip them to change society, working as effective collaborators with others. Temple put it like this in one of his presidential addresses to the association: 'It will be impossible, literally impossible to organise society on the principle of justice until every individual has his capacities developed to the fullest extent, because till then there will always be a conflict between what a man is worth as a matter of fact, in the economic world for example, and what he *might* be worth.'[10] Temple also held that this development should not be an individual thing with one person vying against another, but rather as something done in community. In Temple's submission before the Royal Commission on Oxford and Cambridge in 1920, when he was interviewed as President of the WEA, he spoke of his extreme desire to keep out of (the WEA and University Extension) classes anything of the competitive spirit. It was education for life.

'Don't teach my boy poetry' wrote a dissatisfied father to Temple. 'He's going to be a grocer.' But for Temple, literature, music, history and economics, were all part of education for life that would stretch the capacities of every person who was given the opportunity to engage with them. Yes, theology (not 'Religion') was to be on the curriculum, but theology as part of a dialogue about the Gospel of the Kingdom, and offered (like all subjects) as a conversation, in which the experience of those present in their culture was an ingredient in the process, and not as a didactic presentation. 'To us, theology was not a technical and professional knowledge' wrote Kelly. 'We were studying God's view of human life.'[11]

Temple was hugely influential in creating a new religious climate, and this provided the context for the conversion of C. S. Lewis, acknowledged or not. Lewis commented that he had never had the experience of looking for God, but rather felt that God had stalked him and fired. This was at the age of 30, five years after his election as a Fellow of Magdalen College, Oxford, and following long discussions with his (Roman Catholic) friend, J.R.R. Tolkien, and a few months after William Temple returned to Oxford to do some preaching and teaching. This was 1931, and Temple, then Archbishop of York, was asked to lead the Mission to the University of Oxford, and in his addresses to students in St Mary's Church, he spelt out the backbone of his theology. Faith was presented as a 'hypothesis'; the life of faith is a life of 'testing out'; the end is 'human welfare'. However, this was not an intellectual game, and Temple told his audiences that you can only reach the end by 'inner consciousness' and personal communication with 'Ultimate Reality'. He spoke of the 'Word of God', not in terms of biblical text, but as the word made flesh, and it is to be heard in 'communion'. Creeds are important, but were formed in a cultural context, so the form of words is outdated, but we can say them undertaking to live 'as if' the underlying principle was true. That principle is that God is mysterious, but by acting out 'sacrificial love' in the world, *we are* believing in the Holy Spirit, the diffused power of God discernible everywhere in the Universe; while prayer is not changing the mind of Christ, but seeking the mind of Christ.[12]

All this was at a time when Archbishops were still consulted by statesmen and politicians. In the country at large, his words were heard, but not necessarily with the respect and acceptance of previous generations, though what he was saying was clearly anti-fundamentalist, and Temple had a growing following.

How was Society Changing and what might Christians Hope For?

The social and cultural change between the wars was observed by T. S. Eliot in his series of three lectures given at Corpus Christi College Cambridge, in March 1939, and entitled *The Idea of a Christian Society*.[13] In these he suggested that Britain was now living in a 'neutral' society; no longer Christian in any recognisable form from the past, and poised on the edge of a cataclysmic descent into destruction as the perils of the Pagan (Fascist) society loomed large, the liberal chaos of English society increased, and the Second World War loomed.[14] The self-set question he asked was: How can we understand and respond to the Christian Gospel so that individually we may live our lives to the glory of God, and *corporately* make a Christian Society in the new political, economic and social landscape?

So what did Eliot say?

Industrialisation and social change, together with increasing secularisation, had brought about in England a State with 'a progressive and insidious adaptation to totalitarian worldliness'; sidelining religion as a matter of private belief and morality in private life. Meanwhile in public life, the prevailing culture, and the gap between rich and poor, the haves and the have-nots, was encouraging a culture of avarice in which selfishness and greed would proliferate, having no public moral compass to guide it. Eliot said that he was surprised that the present (pre-1939 war) culture retained so much of traditional morality and behaviour – 'largely unconsciously' he noted – but could not see how this could last.

In a BBC broadcast talk delivered in February 1937 (and later published in *The Listener*) in a series on 'Church, Community and State' Eliot reflected on his own unconscious acceptance of a moral blind spot when he said: 'I am by no means sure it is right for me to improve my income by investing in the shares of a company, making, I know not what, operating perhaps thousands of miles away. And in the control of which, I have no effective voice – but which is recommended as a sound investment…. Where the line is to be drawn between speculation and what is called legitimate investment is by no means clear. I seem to be a petty usurer in a world largely manipulated by big usurers.'[15]

Everyone was somehow being compromised. So what is the 'Idea' of a Christian Society in and beyond this chaos?

Eliot conceptualised 'the community of Christians' as the continuity of fellowship; it was present at national level (but he was sceptical of the 'clerisy') and the local level, where the parish, he deemed, was 'in decay'. But he committed himself to the 'idea' that in a society of multiple identities, there can be a *Christian* society holding the Gospel of the Kingdom at its heart, as the 'core' commitment; although how this will be translated into practical terms, Eliot says he has not the competence, nor the understanding of the global circumstances ahead, to prophesy.

George Every however had two practical offerings: He said that the Church must distinguish between 'God' and Religion and its forms and, by proper (Kelly-like!) theological education, prepare Christians for these future circumstances. Secondly, we do not know what form change will take, but those who are gathered into unity in the sacramental life of the visible Church will produce something of a common mind when the time comes.

The war came and, at the beginning of the war, C.S. Lewis was invited to preach in the University Church, Oxford, and expounded a very Temple-like theme. The whole of life (the every day) is to be lived to the glory of God. 'The works of Beethoven or the work of a charwoman, become spiritual on precisely the same condition, that it is offered to God'. We can't all do the same, but what each does is of equal value. 'A mole must dig to the glory of God and a cock must crow.'[16] In the transformation of lives now, 'poetry replaces grammar, gospel replaces law, longing transforms obedience, as gradually as a tide

117

lifts a grounded ship.'[17] This is Kingdom theology. William Temple wrote something similar in a book he published the following year, 1940; he said, 'It is a great mistake to suppose that God is only, or even chiefly, concerned with religion.'[18]

C.S. Lewis was a pioneer of the kind of broadcast talks that were later to be much promoted, and in them he was reasonable and avuncular – yet always appealing to the imagination. He knew many of his listeners were either estranged from or puzzled by religion, and his talks were punctuated by such phrases as 'If you are thinking of becoming a Christian…' and 'Anyone who is trying to become a Christian…' or 'A Christian Society is not going to arrive until most of us really want it…'. A key question Lewis asked was: Why is it so difficult to feel as one was told to feel about God? In answer he suggests that if we put the Gospel into an imaginary world, and strip it of its stained glass and Sunday School associations, then our feelings might regain their potency. The key is 'imagination'. Later his Narnia books did just that, allowing many generations, in the UK and the United States especially, to revisit something they had lost.

Temple became Archbishop of Canterbury during the war, eleven years after he conducted that influential University Mission in Oxford, and during this time he was consulted in the planning for post-war Britain in both the Education Acts and the creation of the Welfare State. On the occasion of his enthronement as Archbishop of Canterbury, on April 23, 1942, he preached, and used the phrase 'the welfare state.' He said that what they were seeing was the demise of the power state, and what they should be planning for was the creation of a welfare state.

In that same year, 1942, he published *Christianity and the Social Order,* which was a vision of society in a post-war Britain, and a challenging programme for the community of Christians. Here he was developing, in very practical terms, his earlier insight that the task of the Church is to proclaim the Kingdom. He had earlier written, 'The business of the Church is to inspire; it is the business of the nations and their citizens to act on that inspiration in the various affairs of life.'[19]

Temple died in October 1944, and caused a stir even then by being cremated rather than buried. Was this a last signal of his position regarding the resurrection of the 'body'? Even in this time of war, the obituaries, in the popular press as well as the Broadsheets, were fulsome. This tubby gaitered toff had somehow gained a hearing across the boundaries of working class and middle class cultures and identities; and there was a wave of national affection which lingered when Labour under Clement Attlee took power in 1945. Temple had been a party member from 1918 to 1925, and there was much hope that his legacy for social justice would continue to inform both the national agenda and the mission of the Church. At its centre would be the work of education.

Attempts at Structural Church Change to Ensure the Legacy

In 1945 the Church of England did not have a central body dealing with adult education, which was in the hands of the National Society, a voluntary body, who in the previous year had appointed a Commission to report on the Church's role in Adult and Continuing Education. The Chairman was Sir Richard Livingstone, President of Corpus Christi College, Oxford, and also Vice Chancellor of Oxford University. He wrote:

> In the past, intellectual doubts and difficulties affected a small educated class: today through the press and cheap books in one form or another they reach almost everybody; many who in the past accepted traditional beliefs with comparative docility, today find themselves beset by doubts and questions.

The report goes on to say that the neglect of adult education is not confined to the Church, but is a weakness of the nation; now is the time to realise that education is a *lifelong* process.[20]

The report's conclusions were accepted, and in 1947 the Church of England set up an Adult Departmental Council with Richard Livingstone as its Chair. Systematic schemes of adult religious education based on wartime army education schemes proliferated; house-groups, listening groups, the use of radio and television and collaboration with the WEA, Local Authority Education Committees, and University Extra Mural Departments was encouraged. Over the next twenty years, during and following nearly a decade of austerity, the outcomes of the establishment of the National Health Service and the Butler Education Act of 1944, through the Korean War, the early stages of the 'Cold War' and into the Suez crisis of 1956, both the Nation and the Church found themselves working in a new social milieu, as gender roles and traditional attitudes to work, leisure and family, began to change. In the next decade, the pace of change escalated with television, the pop/youth culture; everyone had a TV and telephone, and more people owned cars, motor bikes or scooters.

Lady Chatterley and Beyond

In 1960, John Robinson, by then Bishop of Woolwich, was called as a defence witness by Penguin Books who had published a full text of *Lady Chatterley's Lover* by D. H. Lawrence. He supported its publication, and said it presented sex as a sort of Holy Communion. The Press headlined that he said it was a book 'all Christians should read.' Three years later came *Honest to God*, which is where we began, and that book, with its successor *But that I Can't Believe* and a host of other books of challenge, caused immense excitement among both the young and adult population. I have briefly described what we did at Kelham following the publication of *Honest to God*, but it is also worth noting that my father, who worked in Woolwich Arsenal, told me of the immense interest in that book in his generation among members of the South London Industrial Mission. But for the young especially, the liturgical freedom to experiment outside the confines of the Church of England's prescribed texts was liberating and offered for them a *world-embracing* holiness. Parish priests up and down the country hosted groups which offered a dialogue about, rather than instruction on, God. They preached on the changing times, what the Church was about, and prayer. However, both the Archbishop of Canterbury (Michael Ramsey) and C. S. Lewis (just before he died) signalled their disapproval of *Honest to God* and (seemingly) the tide of energy and experimentation that it had brought.

Patterns of corporate worship had already changed as the 1960s advanced. Gabriel Hebert, biblical and liturgical scholar, had pioneered the 'Parish and People' initiative, having been inspired in the 1930s by the Roman Catholic liturgical movement in France. In 1962 I accompanied him to France to revisit churches on the Left Bank (St Severin and St Germaine de Pres) to see how they had developed. Then we went to Taizé, meeting with Brother Roger and Max Thurian and staying with that innovative, ecumenical Community before visiting the seminary of the 'Mission de France'. There Father Gabriel was given the bedroom of the Cardinal Protector of the 'Mission'. The bed was a four poster with a red Cardinal's hat hanging over it. Modesty would not allow him to use it, so he had my small room while I enjoyed delusions of grandeur. Gabriel then gave a paper on the Jewish foundations of the Eucharist while we stayed at the Abbey of Bec, taking part in a symposium on worship. Excitement and change were in the air. The Roman Catholics were preparing for Pope John XXIII's Council, and we gathered at the local *auberge* in the evenings with members of the symposium including Père Louis Bouyer[21] who was a leading academic preparing for the forthcoming Vatican II Council.

The changes of the wider church penetrated the monastic walls of Kelham. We returned from France to Kelham, and Gabriel died soon after, but George Every guided his own version of Gabriel's reforms through the Chapter, replacing the old High Mass, and daily private masses for each priest, with a corporate daily Eucharist round the altar, together with a weekly sermon. Several of us worked with Nottingham Social Workers in a project for the socially isolated called 'Friendship Unlimited', known to one and all as FU, while others worked with students in Childrens' Homes as part of the new curriculum. As Empire receded and immigration increased, we were involved with 'Nottingham International', gaining support and finance and the beginnings of a 'needs agenda' for an International Cultural Centre to provide resources for the tide of commonwealth immigrants who were changing the city. Similar activity burgeoned in towns and cities up and down the nation, although rather less in the countryside.

Maintenance or Mission?

However, during the late 1960s a reaction had already set in and there was a movement to withdraw from joint Church/State/Voluntary provision of any kind. There was a drive towards *parish based* learning groups to build up a new, better-informed and energetic clerisy within church walls, and many schemes of that sort flourished. Clerisy (a word invented by Coleridge to mean an intellectual elite or vanguard) was corrupted and used at the time (by those against it) to describe an in-group of clergy and laity who controlled the agenda in diocese and parish, as they sought to reassert what they regarded as traditional practice. As this happened, courses on religious subjects in WEA districts in Great Britain were declining: 1967 – 181, 1968 – 166, 1969 – 138; and so it went on, with similar withdrawal from other joint projects during the 1970s. At the very time when the general public's interest in God and the Church had been stimulated by John Robinson and others, and a wide range of people from war veterans to teenagers were being stimulated to look at 'worldly holiness' in a new way, the leadership in the churches was urging a withdrawal from general adult education with its potential to exert a profound influence, narrowing the frontiers, and retreating into a domestic agenda, and domestic institutions.

The 1960s ended with 'stagflation,' too much money chasing too few goods, an oil crisis, and industrial unrest. In the Church, there had been a dramatic fall in the number of those coming forward for ordination, and there was an economy drive to save money as prices rose. At local level, grand rectories and vicarages were sold, and theological colleges (some no longer financially viable) were closed or merged. In addition, the Church Colleges of Education similarly came under review, with threat of merger and/or closure, and another major institution that represented the Church *in* Society was weakened. Edna Mallet, a member of the Company of the Sacred Mission with many years teaching experience in South Africa with the Society, wrote of the opportunities in Church Colleges of Education, which were at that time assisting in the training of 13,000 teachers. The opportunities for serious religious education were enormous; but, she feared, were not being properly appreciated or grasped. She quotes a college chaplain who wanted to see 'the chapel fostering concern for every part of life in the world, encouraging criticism and drawing attack if need be.' She commented: 'He gets plenty poor man, but then his motto is "better a hotbed than a hothouse."' [22] We knew how he felt.

We had the Experience but Missed the Meaning

Harold Wilson was Prime Minister of the United Kingdom from 1964 to 1970 and from 1974 to 1976. An academic and an economist, his (Labour) Government was credited with passing some much needed social change. Laws concerning divorce, censorship, homosexuality, abortion and immigration helped change the face of Britain; and while some legislation was controversial, much was supported by the church, and was certainly not anti-religious in intent. However, partly because within the church there were those who regarded all these changes negatively, and they got the ear of the press, but partly just because of the change in culture, there was a significant 'distancing' between church and people.

Wilson was concerned to shape the economy for the new age, and to do so he tampered with the church calendar. Easter occurs at varying times, with Whitsun fifty days after. He decided that the economy needed a fixed spring break, regardless of the ecclesiastical calendar, and separated the Whitsun Bank Holiday from the Whitsun Christian Feast day. This had the effect of dismantling an aspect of national shared culture. Since at least the early years of the twentieth century, the Whitsun break had been part of the cultural life of the country. Only the elderly will now remember the shut-down in business life with Whit walks, processions, Whit fairs, cricket matches, coach trips, and 'church'. At Kelham the car park filled with charabancs with visitors wearing Whit Bonnets, to watch cricket, picnic, play games – and attend Festal Evensong. Before the end of the decade, most of this had disappeared, and the church colluded (unintentionally) by returning to the more theologically correct term 'Pentecost' for this season. 'Pentecost Weekend' does not sing in the same way as the old 'Whit,' and a lively connection between the liturgical calendar and ordinary life was lost. This was representative of the widening gap between church and society.

At this time, an ecumenical initiative was taken by Canon Stephen Burnett (1914–91), Adult Education Officer at Church House Westminster, who gathered his Roman Catholic, Baptist, URC and Methodist 'opposite numbers' (or as near as it was possible to get) to form a voluntary Association which would take on the Temple agenda in the light of official denominational lack of leadership. The Christian Association for Adult and Continuing Education (CAACE, pronounced 'khaki') in the 1970s gathered a network of practitioners country-wide to pursue what building on Temple's educational legacy and the Robinson popular theological initiative might look like, and how it might be delivered. The Central Committee (Chair, Stephen Burnett, Church of England) was made up of the national post-holders in the major Churches: Methodist, Roman Catholic (the 'laity Commission') and the United Reformed Church. I was excited to be a part of it.[23] Working through our respective networks and sharing ideas and programme initiatives, together with national and regional ecumenical conferences, we tried to alert the Church to the need for change, and offer user friendly resources that could be implemented at local level to bring as many people aboard as possible. Conferences in Europe with both Roman Catholic and Protestant networks of a similar kind opened our eyes and informed our minds to what was clearly an international movement.

There was a boost in 1973 when the Russell Report to the Government on Adult Education was published, recognising the need for continuing education for people in their roles as parents, carers, employers and employees as well as skills education for both professionals and volunteers running youth clubs, and doing work with disabled people and other work in the community. Collaboration with Voluntary Organisations, especially the Churches, was urged, and many good initiatives were pioneered over the next decade.[24]

But while we had encouragement, and much good work was done, we were still treading ground. In spite of many experiments in 'good practice' and local buoyancy, events in the wider world, and a lack of urgency and consistency within the Churches, meant that the dominant agenda was maintenance, not mission; there was a withdrawal into congregation building, and less contribution to the common good of society at large. We knew we were at the end of an 'era' and we were trying to prepare for a new and challenging period ahead; but there was no 'Wittenberg moment.'[25] In fact I was to conclude that what lay ahead was more than the transition from one of Dawson's 'ages' to another; it was an epoch change that would take us into new territory.

Adolf Von Harnack, the prominent German Lutheran church historian and theologian, wrote in his book *What is Christianity?* (1901):

> There are only two possibilities ... either the Gospel is in all respects identical with its earliest form, in which case, it came with time and departed with it; or else it contains something

which under different historical forms is of permanent validity.[26]

We shall now move to consider what forms those might be.

CHAPTER 6

From Adaptionism to Radicalism

'When you hear the sound of marching in
the tops of the balsam trees, then bestir
yourselves.'
(2 Samuel 5:27)

Challenges

In the mythical story told in the second book of Samuel,
the Israelites are in a pickle and they are told to be on
the alert to take action. It will take the form of an angelic
army (code for the energy of God), spurring them to
wake up. In this chapter we will look at some recent
Anglican history to illustrate not only the widening gap
between church and society but also the increasingly
inward-looking nature of the Church, especially from
the 1980s onwards.[1] This history may be a spur to us to
'wake up' and bestir ourselves.

In 1986, Timothy Raison,[2] a village neighbour,
asked me to help organise and take part in a seminar
between some senior politicians and church leaders at

Christ Church, Oxford. It all arose from a Report which Archbishop Runcie had commissioned and which was published in that year under the title *Faith in the City*. Far more prescient and far seeing than he is often given credit for, Runcie was driven by his own realisation of the secularisation of the values of our cities, and of the suffering and alienation of huge numbers of people, de-skilled and driven into poverty. The Report addressed both church (as the Established Church of the land) and the State, at that time headed by Margaret Thatcher and a Conservative government. It was highly critical of government policies, and Timothy Raison, said to me one day 'The lady is disturbed. She cannot understand why the Church is providing consistent opposition to the government, and this report is the last straw. Shall we organise a seminar, and produce something that she can take aboard?'

I had read the report, but now studied it in close detail, and found it had been put together with the meticulous foresight and careful preparation that the Archbishop gave to such issues. It had been chaired by Sir Richard O'Brien, a distinguished civil servant who for six years had chaired the Manpower Services Commission, and also included people at a local level, such as the Vice Chair of Sheffield City Council, and significant experienced representatives of other Christian traditions and other faiths. No government enquiry could have been better composed to provide a balanced report. It contained thirty-two recommendations to the Church of England, and twenty-three for the Government to consider.

At the heart of the report was the conviction that a growing number of people were excluded by poverty or powerlessness from sharing the common life of the nation. Further it observed that the ethics which formed the nation's common life was changing, and that (as T.S. Eliot had feared) altruism was being replaced by egotism, a sense of community by self esteem, and the practice of charity by greed. Some of the blame for this was laid at the Government's door, hence the tensions between the Church and the Conservative government. For the report triggered enormous publicity, and public questioning of the ethics of many Thatcherite policies with regard to the issues raised in the report – about homelessness, taxation, 'care in the community', child benefit, law enforcement and much more.

In addressing the Church, the report underlined that it must be a 'church for the poor' whereas it was often still driven by 'secular attitudes to power and class which persist in subtle and not so subtle ways.' The Church was encouraged to address the education of the clergy and its leaders (whose training was regarded as inadequate and inappropriate), become a much more *local* church, and share its buildings in whatever way possible to serve the surrounding community, 'like someone opening the door of her home.' For some of us, this was the kind of lead for which we had been hoping; whereas for the government it was seen as the work of 'meddling clerics,' who should keep out of politics, sing hymns and go to tea parties.

For our meeting in Oxford, it was my role to recruit half a dozen leading church thinkers, and Tim would bring half a dozen senior politicians. We would meet at Christ Church Deanery (by kind invitation of the Dean, Eric Heaton) in the afternoon, and work through until evening, with breaks for tea and dinner. The clerical team included Rowan Williams, recently appointed as Lady Margaret Professor of Divinity at Oxford, Richard Harries, then Bishop of Oxford, the Dean himself, David Nicholls of St Anthony's College, Oxford, and a former lecturer in economics in the University of the West Indies (who famously kept a parrot called The Archdeacon) and myself. Among the politicians was Douglas Hurd, who had just become Home Secretary.

When it was time to break for dinner, David Nicholls had just made the point, quoting from *Faith in the City*, that the church was a church for the poor. The college butler announced dinner, and we went into the dining room where the table had been set with grand candles and ornaments from the College's historic silver. At the doorway, Douglas Hurd paused and looked at the splendid table and said to us *sotto voce* 'Ah, I see what you mean; a church for the poor !' Of course he was wryly underlining the dilemma of the Established Church, which Trollope had described so poignantly in *The Warden* in the mid-nineteenth century. We were still facing it over a hundred years later, in 1986. I am not sure that our short meeting did anything at all to lessen the antagonism that Margaret Thatcher felt from the Church – or vice versa – but, in that moment of walking into dinner, I felt keenly a sense of the paradoxes we faced as the Established Church, and began to understand that some serious nettles had to be grasped.

Thirty years later, now in 2016, this sense of dilemma is still a part of the church's crisis. 'Good' men and women are caught up in a system in which sacrificial decisions taken at the personal and local level do not necessarily make things better for the victims of social injustice, or model without ambiguity the kind of church that would take their loyalty and commitment. It is not without a deep searching of his/her own identity that a person can put on a mitre. *'Nolo episcopari'* was the ancient cry: *'I don't want to be a bishop.'* When a person takes on the role of bishop, archbishop or pope for that matter, then that person loses some personal freedom. They are imprisoned by the institution, and people do not understand when they say 'As I person I think this; but acting as bishop I must do that.' When there is a clash between the two then there is often ambiguity, which can be taken as indecision or lack of integrity.

Choices

'An Archbishop who Nailed his Colours to the Fence?'[3] This oft-repeated description of Robert Runcie in the Lambeth 1988 period was not one that I recognised or agreed with, at least in relationship to the early years of his archepiscopate, or indeed when it was made while preparations for the Conference were taking place. These years with Robert Runcie at the helm were when I found myself drawn irresistibly towards a more radical version of change than I had previously thought necessary or possible, and he was giving a lead. In commissioning the *Faith in the City* report, he attempted to get the church to do something about the increasing gap between poor and rich as many perceived it; one result was that the traditionally cordial relationship between the Conservative party and the Church of England was eroded to some degree, and the Church of England could no longer be called 'the Tory party at prayer.' The Report gave a voice to inner-city churches; it led to the foundation of the Church Urban Fund (1988) which eventually raised and gave out 55 million pounds for faith initiatives in the inner city; and it was a beacon of hope to many in deprived, inner-city areas.

Nevertheless, the larger question of *what the church was to be* was still largely unasked and unanswered. Anthony Russell, Chair of the Education and Training Council in the Diocese of Oxford, of which I was the Director in the 1980s, had suggested three ways forward in his 1980 book *The Clerical Profession*.[4] When I read his book, I realised that within it he had set out a map that many would recognise, and a future we should explore. He wrote of three possibilities for the church of the future. First, there was the church of the traditionalist future in which, in spite of falling numbers, there is an attempt to keep the church structure with the clerical profession at its centre, as it had developed in the late nineteenth and twentieth centuries, concentrating on its liturgical role, even if its pastoral reach was reduced. Second, there was the church of the adaptionist future; recognising that change was part of the church's mode of being in history. Here, I was horrified to be able to identify myself. I had slipped back from earlier challenge into continuing to embrace and initiate change, of course, but in a diocesan role, edging forward, trying to carry as many people as possible into new forms of ministry, laity empowerment, the ordination of women, and educational programmes – in other words, being satisfied with making gradual progress towards a Kingdom church. The details of Russell's third category – the church of the Reformist future – did not engage me. It was recognising myself in that 'middle' category, as an *adaptionist*, that moved me to a new position; or rather to a former position from which I was in danger of lapsing. The future of the church demanded *radical* change.

Communion at Crossroads

In 1988 Archbishop Runcie convened what he knew would be a crucial gathering of the Anglican Communion in the form of the Lambeth Conference – a gathering of bishops.[5] Since its inception in 1867, this Lambeth Conference had been gathering every ten years, called and presided over by the Archbishop of Canterbury. It is not, and never has been, a legislative assembly but, rather, a meeting of friends with a common history, who meet to share problems, exchange insights, and seek a common mind and voice on issues facing society and the church.

Runcie was keenly aware of the changes in the Communion that de-colonisation had brought, with many newly created dioceses in Africa and Asia, whose bishops' theology often reflected the missionary society of their origin – a global spread of the 'broad church' that is the Church of England. The previous Lambeth Conference, in 1977, had been presided over by Archbishop Donald Coggan, and retained much of the 'old style', dominated by English and American bishops, with the Archbishop gathering them round a piano in the evenings for a sing song. Runcie knew the landscape had changed, would change more, and that the re-shaping would be crucial if the Communion was to flourish in this new world.

With an understanding of the changing nature of the Anglican Communion, there had been attempts to foster understanding between its different provinces and dioceses. For example, 'Partners in Mission' was a Runcie initiative, encouraging English dioceses to partner with overseas dioceses to discover what they could exchange at grass roots level that would enhance their understanding and support of each others' needs in relation both to church and society. But it was not only the Anglican Communion that had changed in the intervening ten years; so had relations with other churches. Runcie had long carefully nurtured relationships with the Eastern Orthodox Churches, and from his appointment as Archbishop had worked hard at creating better theological understanding with the Church of Rome, culminating in the setting up of ARCIC, the Anglican/Roman Catholic Joint International

Commission, exploring what theological agreements might be made towards closer union. Progress had been made, and another report was due from that body in 1990.

It was in this spirit of mutuality that Robert Runcie began to construct the style and substance of his Conference. The background booklet for the Conference was called *Open to the Spirit.*[6] As the editor, Colin Craston, said in his introduction: 'The preparation for Lambeth is a family preparation' in which listening to one another is vital. The aim of the essays was to 'stimulate discussion, point up the questions, and possibly indicate some signposts.' Both Runcie and the Anglican Consultative Council (ACC) were aware of the huge cultural differences in regard to issues such as gender – and Craston gently commented in his introduction to the book: 'The original intention had been to have several women contributors. In the end just one was possible. Grace Gitari, writing from an African culture traditionally male dominated, tells how she sees renewal affecting man-women relationships for the greater freedom in Christ of both.' Whatever story lies behind the comment 'Just one was possible,' it was a prescient insight into what was to come.[7]

I was appointed as *Process Consultant* to the Conference, to take a lead in planning and executing what the Archbishop considered a key change in the Conference style. It now had 800 bishops attending, some of whom did not speak English and had never been outside their country of origin. All bishops were asked to 'bring their Diocese to Lambeth', setting before the conference the faith and order issues on their minds. These would form part of the agenda, which now had group work as the main part of the conference, interleaved with plenary sessions, against a daily background of bible studies prepared by Bishop John Taylor.[8]

Each morning began with a meeting of the Primates, the Archbishops of the various Provinces of the Communion, as they planned the business of the day. I was present at all of these sessions, and watched as Robert Runcie, with Desmond Tutu and Robert Eames, then the Primate of Ireland, imaged the 'we are a family' model, getting to know their colleagues, shaking hands, and listening and sharing. In the evenings, there were lighter moments as well, presided over by a brother of SSM, Austin Masters, who had worked for many years in the Province of South Africa. The Conference also had time for informal groupings, and one evening I found myself invited to a group with some English, American and African bishops to discuss the ordination of women, and the Episcopal Church's 'lurch' (as it was described) towards 'liberal' theology and 'non-biblical' ethics. It was clearly an 'anti-women' group and included the former Episcopal Chaplain at Dartmouth College, my host there in 1967, and now a bishop. I counted him as a friend but it appeared we had very different ideas on this subject. I now found myself listening to views I found disturbing – but more, attitudes about 'difference,' in sexuality for example, which were frankly shocking. The changes the Communion was facing were going to be harder nuts to crack than perhaps anyone had thought.

Lambeth Legacy

At the final plenary session, I had to speak to the assembled bishops on 'Taking Lambeth back to your diocese', and did so immediately before the Archbishop's powerful summary of the conference, with his vision of a changed Universal Church in the process of healing historical divisions, and in doing so providing a model for a divided, dangerous world.[9] I had prepared an evaluation form for the bishops to record their impressions of the value of the Conference, and there was time for this to be done in groups, so that the less confident, and those not used to such written responses (in English) might be helped by those who were. The meeting comprised 61 per cent of participants from the Northern Hemisphere, 21 per cent from Africa and 18 per cent from the rest of the world. As the *Church Times* reported, the process of the conference was certainly dominated by Northern and Western methodology and did not take enough account of the cultural insights of the other parts of the world. This was reflected in the responses on the evaluation forms, and in November the *Church Times* published the results on its front page with the headline 'Lambeth '98 Should be "Less English"'.[10]

The *Lambeth Daily*, circulated throughout the conference to everybody, had an article in the final edition of the Conference about one of the subject area groups that had completed its report. The 'Dogmatic and Pastoral Concerns' group was quoted as follows:

Anglicanism has always embraced a variety of theological opinions within a fundamental unity of faith and order. We believe this comprehensiveness in the past has served well the purpose of the Gospel. Yet in a rapidly changing world many people find diverse interpretations disturbing, and strongly authoritative forms of belief appeal to some even when the same forms repel others. Many Anglicans are confused as to what they ought to believe about, for example, the Virginal Conception, the Resurrection of Christ and the Fatherhood of God. What authority has the Bible? Can credal affirmations from the first Christian century have relevance for the twentieth century? The ethical teaching of Jesus is also widely questioned...

Some ethical questions were debated in a penultimate plenary when the Rt Revd Paul Moore, Bishop of New York, proposed a motion to pledge support to victims of AIDS and to remove discrimination against homosexual people. This was expected to be carried by the 'management' of the Conference, but this motion and others concerning the social order, were challenged in what the *Lambeth Daily* called a 'lively debate', and while the direction of all the motions remained, they were all blunted by amendments from fundamentalist 'Global South' bishops. A third warning sign was that one bishop was reported as having done his homework faithfully, studied the pre-Conference books, and consulted the leaders of his diocese on a long list of issues that he 'brought to Lambeth'. He then found himself confined for most of the conference in a topic group discussing the ministry of the laity, most of which was not applicable to his diocese, people or country. What was he going to take back? Another who had been a bishop for only six months, spent most of his time trying to find out what was going on, because none of the documents was in a language he could understand. A fourth warning sign was signalled by the Brazilian Bishop, Luiz Prado, pointing to his country's poverty, lack of literacy, housing and health care. This was the agenda he had brought. The question of how Lambeth had helped him was left in the air.

The intentions, preparations, staff work, and sheer hard work of the Core Primates, were significant in making this first 'new type Lambeth' a significant occasion.

But it had its failures as well as its successes; what was discovered in its failures as well as what was agreed should have been part of its legacy. The structures of the Communion and its civil service had become more directive. Such a big Communion needed to be 'managed' it was thought, but this too stored up enormous problems for the future. In 1991 George Carey became Archbishop of Canterbury, and made the Communion a priority. However, the complexity of the issues revealed at the Conference, together with its continuing outcomes, proved difficult for the new Lambeth team to grasp.

Mind the Gap

Back in 1988, the metallic voice of London Underground's warning to disembarking passengers had penetrated the mind of most of us at Lambeth. I told Archbishop Runcie of my informal meeting with the 'anti-women' group, and also that my former host at Dartmouth, now a diocesan bishop, had invited me to lead his clergy conference in 1989. 'Go' he said, and get out among as many of them as possible, and come and see me when you get home'. I did as he suggested, and found that while my host bishop had his supporters, there were among the diocesan clergy many who were not, and during my stay, in many deep conversations, I heard the agonised and passionate anxiety of a church that was becoming deeply divided. That informal sample, gathered in a theologically conservative diocese, brought me to the conclusion that the majority did not support the bishop, though many found this distressing. If that was so in this diocese, it might be that the reasoned theology of the Hooker tradition would carry the day in the Episcopal church as a whole. Any lingering doubts in my own mind about the ordination of women were now dispelled, and I told Archbishop Runcie so. I got the impression he was fine about that for me, but not for him, in his role as Archbishop. Meanwhile the theological stirrings of Bishop Spong aggravated the split, and public quarrels among Episcopal congregations began to poison the debate, the atmosphere of parts of the Church, and of course its relationship with others in the Communion.

By the time the evangelical George Carey had become Archbishop of Canterbury (in 1991), an unforeseen legacy of the Runcie years emerged, and that was the strengthening of the 'centre' of the Anglican Communion in order to bring coherence to an increasingly diverse Communion. The Anglican Consultative Council, with the Secretary-General leading a team of a couple of dozen support staff, had become a kind of mini curia, a management centre which Runcie had encouraged in order to keep the burgeoning Communion together. This centralising effect would have repercussions for the Lambeth Conference of 1998, as some tried to turn it into a body which could pass resolutions which were binding across the Anglican Communion – something that was in fact impossible, as the separate provinces have always been independent. But this idea came to be challenged in the search for uniformity rather than simply unity. The question was now not only 'what kind of church should we be?' but also 'what kind of Communion should we be?'

The Lambeth Conference of 1998 was divisive and distressing to many. The staff team had been keen to focus on Third World Debt and its relief, and to develop the pattern of Lambeth '88, fundamentalists in African and Asian churches, as well as some American and British churches, were determined to ensure that Lambeth '98 would brand homosexuality a 'sin', with the 'gay issue' and the authority of the Bible dominating the Conference. In spite of a low profile from the American Bishops, skilful chairing by Archbishop Eames and careful drafting by Bishop Richard Harries, the issue was tabled in a fair minded resolution to allow continuing discussion. This was whittled away by a succession of amendments, which resulted in the Archbishop accepting the resolution 'Lambeth 1.10'. which rejected 'homosexuality' and gay sexual relationships of any sort as 'sinful'. And while assuring gay people that they were loved by God, marriage was out of the question. In the heat of the debate, the Archbishop allowed the insertion of the prefatory words 'While rejecting homosexual practice as being incompatible with Scripture…' and this brought to the surface the underlying battle, which was about biblical authority. A coalition of bishops had come to Lambeth with minds made up, not prepared to listen, and were ready to walk out if Resolution 1.10 were not passed. It was passed with a huge majority. So the case for Lesbian and Gay members of the church to be fully included in its life had been rejected, and although a number of English bishops, and others from around the globe made a pledge to 'reflect, pray and work' for such inclusion, it was a damage limitation exercise. It was devastating news for many of us, and we were left disorientated.

Richard Holloway, a student at Kelham with me in the 1950s and, at the time of the 1998 Lambeth Conference, Bishop of Edinburgh and Primate of the Episcopal Church in Scotland, resigned his office as a result, and at a press conference held on a boat on the Thames, he gave reasons for his resignation and threw his mitre into the waters.[11] He left the institution of the church and continued to explore the mysteries of the cosmos and humanity, both intellectually and in his loving concern for people.

As was inevitable, positions hardened. The Episcopal Church in the USA discerned its direction, and consecrated a (divorced) gay bishop, Gene Robinson; immediately demands for the Episcopal Church to be expelled from the Communion came from the Bishops who had led the debates at Lambeth. International and diocesan boundaries were then breached when some Episcopal parishes invited African bishops to become their leaders in place of their own diocesan bishops. There was now overt discord between Anglicans, which dominated the media, and the agenda of the Church of England too.

Re-Imagining the Anglican Communion

George Carey stepped down as Archbishop of Canterbury in 2002 and was succeeded by Rowan Williams, whose first act was to set up a Commission to advise on how the crisis should be faced. The Commission, chaired by Robert Eames, produced The Windsor Report (2004) with the proposal that, because the chaos was damaging public perception, ecumenical relations, and the bonds of affection within the Communion, a pause should be agreed in which all would refrain from further 'provocative actions,' while a mechanism was devised to bring an ordered resolution to the disputes, and provide a framework for understanding Communion membership.

The Commission proposed that all Provinces should enter in to a 'Covenant' – a biblical concept – which was to be a commitment to God and to each member Province to behave and work as a functional international family in a process to discover God's will for all. The shape and structure of the Covenant would be determined by the Anglican Primates. The Anglican Consultative Council (ACC) was asked to convene a small group to prepare a draft covenant to put before the Primates, and I accepted an invitation to be one of the eight members who began work in 2006.

The carefully crafted draft was sent to the Primates meeting in 2007, who responded by insisting on excluding the Episcopal Church, the Canadian Church and others from the ACC, before they would take part in it. While being bitterly disappointed by this, I nevertheless pleaded for the process to continue. I wrote an article in the *Church Times*, arguing that the Anglican Communion was about working together, not unformity of belief on doctrine. The article was given the title: 'It's a Relationship, Not a Doctrinal Quiz'. But there was a loss of energy and patience on all sides, and the editorial in the *Church Times* that week (published on the same page as my article) argued that it was perhaps too hard to hold the Anglican Communion together in an atmosphere of profound disagreement. 'In such an atmosphere, it would be surprising if anyone had the energy for the re-imagining that Vincent Strudwick advocates.'[12]

Despite the cynicism of the *Church Times* editors about my proposal, I continued to be keen that the process of re-imagining the Communion should continue, and I think the force of 're-imagining' had not been appreciated. The Windsor Report had repeatedly referred to Hooker's concept of 'adiaphora' (code for things which are not fundamental to the faith). While people may disagree about them, Hooker argued, they should not be allowed to affect the unity of the fellowship. I suggested the adoption of 'eudiaphora' – 'good difference'. This good difference would be on fundamental issues, where the disagreement was vitally important: while thinking your opponents wrong to hold their view, you nevertheless accepted their good faith and integrity in holding it, and could continue to live and work together in 'Harmonious Dissimilitude', another Hooker phrase, patiently testing out a future together. I think this went down like a lead balloon.

The inevitable happened, a number of Provinces disassociated themselves from the Communion, and formed themselves into a separated group under the acronym GAFCON (Global Anglican Future Conference). Invitations to the Lambeth Conference in 2008 were refused by GAFCON members, so it was a diminished 650 bishops who arrived for a very different kind of Lambeth than the previous one of 1998. It was to be a 'listening Lambeth'. It began with a Retreat, led by Archbishop Rowan Williams. Then in the Conference there were to be no 'Resolutions' thus avoiding attempts to issue edicts that some wished to be binding (which they could not be). The main part of the work was based on the Zulu model of Indaba groups where issues are discussed, listened to, and 'chewed over'. The worship was offered in different languages and cultures, covering the diversity of the Communion. An amazing modelling of the Church's true priorities was expressed in the London procession of Lambeth Bishops in support of the Millennium Development Goals; the bishops were then addressed by the British Prime Minister.

Listening and being open to the Spirit was in continuity with Runcie's Lambeth Conference. This time, in 2008, more questioning was encouraged; the focus was more on 'the world' and there was an eagerness to play a part in discerning and shaping the common good. But some asked whether a church that was so at odds with itself had the moral authority to comment on the world, as it traditionally had. How could it play a part in shaping the common good when it seemed so out of step with the people? Many were horrified by the sight of bishops lining up in the House of Lords to vote against equal marriage, which had so much support in society at large, especially amongst the younger population that the church so desperately wanted to attract. The gap between church and society had widened.

Rowan Williams stepped down in 2012. The next Archbishop, Justin Welby, an evangelical and former oil executive, picked up the task of how to move forward with an 'impaired' Communion, and perhaps re-imagine the church with a different shape. At any rate for many of my friends and colleagues there was the sound of marching in the balsam trees, and it was time to bestir ourselves, for the last decade or so had left little institutional space for the wrestlers.

CHAPTER 7

Cosmic Transformation and Christian Responsibility

Following the Way in an Epoch of Uncertainty

'Christianities are a significant force operating
in Europe and their key aspect is 'belonging'.
Slavica Jakelic[1]

We now turn from the inward-looking politics of the
Anglican Church, and my own experience of those past
few decades within that Church, to the larger global
forces forging the context in which we wrestle, believe
and do church today.

Globalisation has changed the world, and it is no longer
the case that we can rearrange the deck chairs on those
ecclesial vessels that have carried Christianity during
Dawson's 'ages'. We are in an entirely new situation.
Ewert Cousins wrote of a 'second axial period'. He
understood the first axial period to be a formative one
for the human race, through which local tribal society
was changed, and in this change, the great religions

were formed with their beliefs, structures and ethical outcomes, shaping the politics, economy and culture of the succeeding ages. Cousins held that we have now entered a second axial period in which humanity has to rethink its understanding of human society in relation to the cosmos, together with the place and forms of all religions within it.

In the preceding chapters, I have suggested a way of understanding 'God', and following from this a radical revision of the way we make church. Together these change the priorities of our belonging.The transformation of our comprehension of the world and the cosmos is something for which I have no expertise; but I am sure that the churches must attempt to do so by taking account of what scientists, economists and sociologists discover. Have we a role in not just reacting to global change, but having a responsibility to shape it? I believe we have, and we do our theology amidst a 'conjonction des crises' of which we must take account.

World Without End?

The past seventy years have brought new scientific knowledge about planet earth that has transformed thinking about its future, as well as the role of sentient human beings in shaping it. Sixty-five million years ago, disaster struck the planet and the age of the dinosaurs was over, and mammals evolved. It is now clear that all life is related, and inter-dependent, as most of us have accepted for a century and a half, but much more recently there has been scientific confirmation of what were, until relatively recently, theories.

In 1947 it became evident (from fossils and study of differing species) that there had been one super continent that had broken up; and then in 1960 that the present continents were – very slowly – still moving. At the same time, space travel has increased our knowledge of the universes, bringing both more information, and more mystery about the cosmic setting in which life on earth has evolved. Climate change, accelerated by industrialisation, deforestation, and the extinction of certain species has hit the headlines, while flooding and coastal erosion have impacted the every day lives of millions in different parts of the world, and many thousands of people in the United Kingdom.

'World without end?' which Ken Follet has taken as a warning title for his book on climate change, is a mistranslation of a liturgical text, brought into the culture through generations of use in the Church of England's *Book of Common Prayer*.'Glory be to the Father and to the Son, and to the Holy Ghost; As it was in the beginning, is now and ever shall be, world without end. Amen.' 'World without end' was taken from the King James Bible (Ephesians 3:21), an inaccurate version of both the Greek and Hebrew texts from a phrase which expresses the eternity of God – not that of the planet. 'Through endless ages' is a more accurate translation.

The potentially disastrous cosmic ecological future that faces us means that human beings need to rethink their understanding of the world they live in, and the role of humanity in relation to it. We are not 'in charge' of it all, and the creation is not there for the benefit of humankind, as some literal interpreters of the Bible for a long time thought, but we are that part of the creation with the gift of reason, and if we are to have a role in its flourishing, we must recognise our responsibility as stewards, rather than overseers, and take action quickly. A Muslim scholar, Seyyed Hossein Nasr, expresses it like this: 'One can say that nature is nothing but the Divine Reality manifesting itself on the plane of phenomenal existence.' He goes on

> Earth is man's teacher, and man can learn from the order of nature not only quantitatively but also morally, intellectually, and spiritually … the message of different religions concerning that order only enriches the message that is to be heard.[2]

For God and for Gain

This heading – 'For God and for Gain' – at the top of a page in the ledger of a medieval merchant of Prato, heralds the birth of capitalism, which was given a boost when Protestantism embraced the market, within a declared ethical framework in the sixteenth century.[3] In the nineteenth and twentieth centuries when European dominance of the entire planet began, the enterprise, missionary zeal, artistic and scientific creativity of Western culture gradually dominated, sometimes corrupted, and if necessary crushed by force indigenous cultures throughout the Indian sub-continent, Asia and Africa, often denying them their own histories. It was at this point that the foundation for a global economic system was laid.

However, following the destructive political and economic rivalry of the European states, which culminated in the first 'world' war, the political and cultural superiority of the western powers was gradually called into question. When these powers then rearranged the borders of colonial states and set up regimes to govern them, resistance grew in this long subservient part of the globe, and following the end of the second global conflict in 1946 the colonial era was at an end, and there was a 'reckoning' to be addressed.

The Crucible

National boundaries were crafted under Western influence and monarchies were created. Towards the end of the twentieth century some of these monarchies had become dictatorial regimes like Iraq; but beneath the surface of them all was a smouldering resentment that burst into flames through the actions of Saddam Hussein who invaded Kuwait in 1990. The West responded by pushing the Iraqi army back to its borders. At that time they were careful not to go further, but there were already those in the West who were forecasting a 'clash of civilisations' between Islam and the West, and this fear has escalated in the present day.

In 1992 the conservative American Christian (then putting himself up as presidential candidate) Patrick Buchanan published an alarmist book about immigration entitled: *State of Emergency – the Third World Invasion and Conquest of America*[4] warning against the destruction of American cultural identity by the influx of many millions of Hispanics. The so-called clash of civilisations was extended when in 1998 the Saudi-Arabian Osama bin Laden called for a 'holy war'. He said: 'The United States has been occupying the lands of Islam in the holiest places, the Arabian Peninsula, plundering its riches, dictating to its rulers, humiliating its people, terrorising its neighbours, and turning its bases in the Peninsula into a spearhead through which to fight neighbouring Muslim Peoples.'[5] Al Quaeda was born, and in 2001 the twin towers fell.

I was in the USA on 9/11 and driving into Chicago a week later saw a tall office building with placards in the windows spelling 'R-E-V-E-N-G-E'. The perceived threat of weapons of mass destruction by Saddam provided an excuse for the Iraq war, the outcomes of which led to the disintegration of the Middle East into a cockpit of destruction. While some in the West prophesied a war of civilisations, others sought to guard against it. In the next year while teaching in Washington DC, I witnessed a huge peaceful demonstration of Americans with Arab and Asian ancestry in varieties of eastern dress, protesting their loyalty both to their religion and to the USA.

In the UK while there was mainstream Muslim support of a similar kind, at that time rather muted, we began to witness second and third generation Muslims being radicalised, and the Government established a 'Commission for Cohesion and Integration' (reported June 2007) to examine 'Faith difference', and address migration and integration issues.

What few had foreseen was the emergence of Daesh, the so called Islamic State, fanning the flames of Middle Eastern and other conflicts, and providing a high profile more focused alternative for extremists, with its escalating consequences in Syria, Iraq and a host of other states, as well as in Africa; extending its terrorist war into Europe, and increasing to a torrent the refugees from the devastation that it caused.

From Nation State to Market State to Super Market State

As I have described, it was in 2002 that Philip Bobbitt published his substantial book *The Shield of Achilles* describing the nation state in its decline, being transformed into the market state. The nation state had offered a corporate identity and vision, with social stability and coherence, and defence against outside attack. It held a corporate morality within its borders, and of course (the downside) it could attempt to extend its prosperity and influence, if necessary by armed conflict.

However, Bobbitt, in these early days of globalisation, wrote 'So long as the state's legitimacy is a matter of ensuring the welfare of its citizens, then the globalisation and inter-dependence of its economy, the vulnerability and transparency of its security, and the fragility of its cultural institutions will increasingly deny the state its legitimacy.'[6] In other words, the nation state is dying. Between 1985 and 1991, this is what we were witnessing in the dismantling of the Soviet Union, and through glasnost and perestroika – restructuring and openness – with Russia emerging as a federation of fifteen republics, with many in the former union choosing 'statehood' but with some seeking alliance in the European Union. At the same time, that Union developed its ideas of becoming a political super-state with market values. A free market and 'choice' were the watchwords, while at the same time the great Asian super powers, China and India, embraced a new 'super-state identity' with moves towards a free market, in both cases 'controlled' by the political elite.

The European Union had begun with a vision of peace and the growth of 'community'. Jean Monnet, its most significant founder, wrote: 'The real change we are after is not the free flow of goods. It's the change in the relations between people.'[7] For Monnet, the legacy of continuous conflict must lead to a new age of mutual responsibility. However, as Bobbitt pointed out, as the project evolved there was a shift from the basic ethical values of the founders to the 'profit' values of the market state.

At the end of the twentieth century, globalisation entered a new phase with the internet and increasingly rapid communication, which has changed the way all our institutions work. From 2007, President Putin of Russia recognised an opportunity to challenge the dominance of America in the globalised society that was emerging, and began to build a 'super' nation state again, demonstrated in an aggressive way in the Ukraine and Syria. The market nation super-state is revived, with borders marking its sovereignty, an area of 'influence' extending beyond those borders to protect its national interests (Ukraine, for example) and a new version of 'policing within' to promote nationalism, exemplified in Russia by an alliance with the Orthodox Church, and a harsh crackdown on 'dissidents' (political, libertarian, journalistic) who might question its objectives and methods. The alliance with the Orthodox Church is significant, for in spite of the years of persecution under communism, it remained deeply connected with Russian nationalism.

All of this challenges the Western Market hegemony led by the USA; yet at the same time, reason demands that collaboration is needed to tackle what are global problems. Suspicion and mistrust alternate with tentative progress in facing common perils. In the USA the rise of Donald Trump as the eventually victorious Republican presidential candidate in 2016, and in the UK the success of the Brexit campaign in the 2016 referendum about whether Britain should leave the European Union, were both an expression of the loss of identity and belonging that many people felt, as well as a result of the widening gap between rich and poor. Can a nation state stand apart from the super-states and perform its traditional functions? Brexit supporters thought 'Yes'. In other European countries too, this dynamic is being replicated, with its focus on the migration issue. For everybody, the increase of terror attacks, and the change to the corporate psyche that such attacks have brought about, has subtly changed the everyday habits of many, as well prompting dissatisfaction with the democratic political consensus. The democratic status quo in the political institutions of the West is under question and review.

Volkerwanderung – or Barbarian Invasions?

It was at the end of the fourth century that effective governance came to an end in the Roman Empire, hastened by vast movements of people motivated by social chaos and fear, local conflicts, economic deprivation and often a sense of grievance at the disparity between the poor and the wealthy. There was violence and wanton destruction. When I studied history in the 1950s, these movements of people were still labelled 'the barbarian invasions', which of course carries the message that a lot of nasties swamped the civilisation of the Roman Empire. The four centuries following were called 'saeculum obscura', or the dark ages, because of the scarcity of records, and the period's complexities remain to be discovered. It is to the problematic labelling of this period that I think it is helpful to return, as we attempt to understand the refugee/migrant crisis, and the reaction to it, that confronts the world of the twenty-first century. Are we doing some 'problematic labelling' again, in the way we think of those entering our country?

Towards the end of the last century we were aware of the growing international presence in the UK. At the Department for Continuing Education at Oxford University, where I taught, in response to requests, we put in place a training course, staffed by tutors drawn from the main religions, for marriage counsellors to learn the rules and customs of people from these backgrounds who were increasingly asking for help. With a colleague from the Islamic Centre, Dr Basil Mustafa, we offered jointly seminars for the Oxford Diocesan clergy on 'Understanding Islam'. By 2005 there were 10 million Muslims in Europe, and their numbers were growing. Angelina Jolie-Pitt, Special Envoy for the United Nations Refugee Agency, estimated that, in 2015 alone, over one million migrants entered Europe mainly from Syria, Afghanistan, Iraq, Kosovo, Pakistan, Iran, Nigeria and Ukraine.

Because of the fears of the loss of national identity and economic disaster, there are those who wish to treat both refugees and migrants as barbarian invaders. Borders must be closed to stop the flow. It is increasingly clear that this is not just a problem for the European Union, or for the United Kingdom, and closed borders will not solve it. It is a crisis that affects the whole world, and it is not transitory. At the time of the financial crisis of 2010, Rowan Williams – then still Archbishop of Canterbury – reminded us that the word 'economy' is the Greek word for housekeeping, and not an abstruse discipline that only experts can understand. If we have a global economy, then housekeeping is no longer a matter that individual nation states can solve for themselves alone; we need a common policy. There is no opt out and it is already becoming the role of the churches, and of leaders in all the great faith communities, to hold before political and economic elites the message that the world's housekeeping depends on the participation of us all.

Are faith communities up to the task of prioritising this role as basic to their *raison d'être*? The traditional structures of 'religion' are not, but the Pope has woken everybody up with his 2016 encyclical *Laudato si'*. Translated as 'Praise be', these are words taken from St Francis of Assisi's prayer for the whole creation of which we are part. 'All praise be yours O sister earth who sustains and governs us…' It is a priority the Pope invites us to understand so we can carry out our role as stewards of the natural world, part of which is ensuring justice for the poorest and most vulnerable. He calls for the transformation of political and economic systems to ensure this. Will he be heard?

The cork cannot be put back in the bottle, and the number of Muslims already identifying as 'belonging' in Europe has curiously helped to challenge the post-Christian secular identity and ethical outcomes that seemed to have become embedded in the market states. Europeans are asking again: 'Who are we?' A group of politicians and academics meeting in Vienna, on the initiative of a former President of the European Commission Signor Romano Prodi, concluded that 'markets cannot produce a politically resilient solidarity.'[8]

Those who then say that a revival of religious nationalism cannot produce this either are also right, for the churches' diversification in Europe (in Poland and Serbia to take but two examples) would lead to an intensification of divisions. Tribal religion has given and can give rise to the most bloody conflicts. However, increasingly de-institutionalised expressions of Christianity, along with the ecumenical and inter-faith cooperation that has been developing in the last fifteen years, may be creating the momentum in the long term to challenge seemingly intransigent forms of religious division. Islam has brought religion back into the public place and it has helped to bring back a transformed version of Christianity with it. Whether religion can capture the European (including the UK) mindset and imagination is now being put to the test.

The Eye of a Needle – the Notion of Possible Impossibility: a change in the relationships between people

In the 'Prelude' I asked the reader to listen to a poem by Seamus Heaney in which a question is asked: 'How shall a rich man enter the Kingdom of God through a needle's eye?'There is reference here to a passage in three of the gospels in which Jesus says to a rich man asking how he might be saved:'Again I tell you, it is easier for a camel to go through the eye of a needle than for someone who is rich to enter the kingdom of God.'[9] It has long been claimed (since at least the fifteenth century, but possibly as early as the ninth century) that the Needle's Eye was the name of a gate into Jerusalem which looked impossible for a heavily laden camel to negotiate, but was known to have been successfully negotiated by experienced, clever and innovative drovers. Whether this was actually the case or not, the story is a good one for our purposes. It suggests a possible impossibility.

I have argued for a plural society. Not multi-cultural, but plural, always recognising the tension between differences in some ethical areas, while working for the common good of the society of which we are a part. The market value of 'self at the expense of the other', is alien to faith communities who together work to safeguard gracious humanity. 'Minority' concerns, and how these may be justly addressed and celebrated within a plural society, will be part of the offering, which together we explore at the local level and commend to civil society, as the Pope has done. In the competing voices seeking to be heard searching for belonging and identity, the followers of all religions need to be like clever innovative camel drovers, building on their experience of the recent past.

In the UK, Anglican churches are working locally with ecumenical partners and members of other religions in respectful difference, uniting in what is common for them all in collaborating for the common good. How this will develop and progress in this era of instant communication is still part of an evolving process outlined in the last two chapters. However it is on the basis of this growing experience that we may look back to the Apostolic age and renew our commitment as 'people of the Way.' Christopher Dawson wrote that in the first age of the church the disciples were creating something absolutely new. Changes in the global landscape, and its politics and economy, mean that Christians have to inspire something similar in the UK and in Europe at large.

In an essay on 'The Church of England the Common Good', Malcolm Brown, Director of Mission and Public Affairs for the Church of England, writes that in England:

> the optimistic outcome would be the emergence of a public politics and a new economics in which the common good featured strongly as a governing theme congruent with Christian social theology and which maintained a place for the churches and religion more generally within its conception of what a good society might look like.[10]

If the Kingdom/Trinity model is followed through, there is hope that a good outcome may evolve.

Like those early followers of Jesus in the gospel story we have to launch out into the deep.[11]

CHAPTER 8

Towards a Very Odd Church Indeed

'The space of the Church is not there in order
to deprive the world of a piece of territory but
in order to prove to the world that it is still the
world which is loved by God.'
Bonhoeffer, *Ethics*

In the final chapter of the *Oxford Illustrated History
of Christianity*, John Taylor wrote on 'The Future of
Christianity' which, he acknowledged, was a chancy
business, because he firmly believed that the shape and
form of a religion in its thought, action and organisation
is affected by what happens in the world of politics,
economics and science.[1] The events of the past quarter
of a century have changed many of the facts and figures
in the geo-political map he was reading, but Taylor quotes
two distinguished Roman Catholics whose judgments
still carry weight in the light of the recent quickening
pace of change. Adrian Hastings wrote of three possible
responses when 'the Vandals are at the gate.' The first is

despair, the second is creating a 'laager' (withdrawing into a cultural defensive huddle), and the third is to imitate St Augustine, and envisage the Church as a catalyst, working in society towards the healing and rescue of the whole. That third option is the theme of my last chapter.

However, that theme involves radical change in the Church as it exists today. Taylor quotes Vincent Donovan, Roman Catholic missionary to the Maasai of Tanzania, saying 'What we are coming to see now, is that there may be many responses to the Christian message which have hitherto been neither encouraged or allowed. We have come to believe that any valid positive response to the Christian message could and should be recognised and accepted as 'Church'. That is, the Church that might have been *and might yet be*.'[2] Clearly there is a question over what he means by 'valid', which will be examined; but what is 'the church that might be?'

The Times, they are a-Changing

In considering Dawson's *Ages of the Church* we have seen how the many responses of making church during the Apostolic age and the first three centuries of following 'the Way,' did indeed produce a variety of responses, some of which remained in the Middle East, and remain (under threat) to this day. Then followed the organisation of Christianity in large blocs – East/West, then Roman Catholic/Protestant – shaping different cultures and 'tribal' groupings in which people learned to understand themselves and how to live their every day lives. Since the Enlightenment, the influences of these blocs on global society at large have diminished. Secularism has increased, and some of the insights gained by wrestlers have made church cultures more porous, and this has led to the questioning and abandonment of some beliefs and practices, and the acquisition of others.

For example, the Christian Church embraced slavery throughout much of its institutional history, and there was a great battle to renounce that moral judgment and practice in the nineteenth century. However, we must also recognise that in spite of that change, we still experience today the persistence of racial social attitudes. The equal place of African-Americans in society continues to be a contentious issue in the USA, in spite of having had an African-American President for eight years. This legacy stems in part from the 'Christian' past, and racism today includes some who claim Christian allegiance (even Biblical authority). In the past, slave owners' reception of Biblical authority for the system, along with long standing custom, colluded to forge their acceptance of slavery.

In our century however, with the benefit of hindsight in the historical story and advances in scientific knowledge, is there any excuse for those who claim to be Christians making such a repugnant moral judgement? Yet such judgments are made, and in the public protest, movements of a disturbed and frightened society, attitudes we had thought were buried, are erupting on our streets.

However, there have always been those (often, though not always, on the margins) who have wrestled with issues, even when those matters have been sanctioned by the Bible and/or institutional religion. As Richard Holloway has pointed out, as early as 1688, Quakers in Pennsylvania did challenge the church's authority. 'Quakers believed in the authority of the inner light, or what we might call conscience. And they knew by the light that guided them that slavery was plain wrong. If all people were of equal value then it was wrong to treat some of them as less than human, as property rather than as children of God. And if the Bible said otherwise, then the Bible was wrong.'[3]

In 1962, in a sermon preached in Canterbury Cathedral, John Robinson appealed against the 'utterly medieval treatment of homosexuals' and asked for 'one more determined push' to get rid of a peculiarly odious piece of sexual hypocrisy. Again it was the Quakers who responded to this call, and in 1963 offered *Towards a Quaker View of Sex* with a reasoned, new inclusive morality.[4]

Nevertheless we have to face the fact that today there are many views on issues such as gender, sexuality, the arms race, patriotism, and the environment, held by some Christians, that make many feel hurt and angry because they are totally contrary to their understanding of the Gospel message. Not only is humanity denied by these contrary views; not only is the Christian voice in society weakened by this lack of unanimity, but because the media is conditioned to expect the Church to be against what most people regard as normal, it is those with such views who are labelled as 'Christian' voices and given the oxygen of the airwaves; just as jihadist terrorists are called Islamists. This means that those associated with religion are often taken – at least in the popular press – to be those with conservative or extremist views, rather than the vast majority of people of faith.

Be Angry, but Sin Not[5]

In the Letter to the Ephesians the author writes about problems in the early Church, and describes the Christian community's disagreements on ethical issues. It is a different list from ours, but at that time equally contentious. The writer warns that when anger at disagreement spills over into abuse and hatred, then we are rejecting the Holy Spirit, the enabler of 'graceful humanity'.

In the early days of the foundation of Kellogg College at Oxford University, where I was and still am a Fellow, I had to entertain our first Honorary Fellow, Umberto Eco[6] with a speech at a formal dinner, and then act as his driver for some other engagements. How would this self-declared secularist relate to an Anglican priest? At his initiative, we began with the personal (we were both born in a vintage year, 1932) and we bonded over that. I had already dissuaded him from smoking between courses at High Table (!) when we were having dinner in college, but now he negotiated that he might smoke in the car as we drove to his engagement. It was the 1990s, and I agreed. Following affirmation and negotiation, we were ready to talk about issues. We tackled some religious issues of the day, in which (having been schooled by Jesuits) he was well informed, and eager to engage in critical debate, with what I can only describe as both passion and respectful curiosity. It was a great lesson in the management of difference for which I was deeply grateful, and in those 'issue conversations' I learned as well as offered. I was reminded of an aphorism of Father Kelly: 'Remember, you're never wholly wrong, unless you think you're wholly right.' In conversation between Christians with whom we disagree, we may have to practise continual listening for a very long time, and as we have seen in the recent history, the Anglican Communion has tried and only partially succeeded at this over deeply divisive and hurtful issues of gender for thirty years.

This long term patient pursuit of mutual understanding is part of my very being. However, I now think, with great reluctance, that the time has come for us – the mainstream majority of the Church – to publicly distance ourselves from those with the 'laager' mentality of biblical fundamentalism, and to cease efforts to keep the structures of the Anglican Communion as they are by including those whose speech and activity is not recognisable as belonging to the embodied Christ. For if we continue in public communion with those exhibiting hurtful and disabling differences, we are giving validity to something we believe not to be valid.

The validity of each among the variety of expressions of Christianity, must depend upon the ability to detect in that expression the same vision of the embodied Christ, present and active, that is the sign of the presence of the Naked God in history and in the world today. In making such a judgement we take a risk, for we know our own vulnerability to error; but if in our conversation we are no longer talking the same language, symbolising or communicating the same vision of God, then the 'communion' is not there. We are sadly recognising a reality. This is not a 'moral high ground'; the failure is ours as well as theirs. Communication does not cease, but – in the case of the Anglican Communion – practical grass roots needs in former partner dioceses are not continually on offer or the hope of renewed dialogue may be given up. In other words, the structures of the present Anglican Communion are no longer those that serve the gospel. The Communion has to be reimagined – and, as events unfold, the Church of England too.

In the fateful year 1963, Peter Sellers starred in a movie entitled *Heavens Above!* lampooning the Church in the guise of a liberal Vicar, whose lack of boundaries sees him launched into space. The Church is not in space, but exists in the reality of everyday life, and needs markers (not walls) to ensure that being 'porous' to the real world does not mean that its fundamental nature is destroyed either by secularisation from without or religiosity from within. The markers of Baptism and the Eucharist are important for wrestlers if they risk the faith journey, for they represent commitment to the journey and belonging to the community. Within the Christian denominations we may begin to view these markers in an even more porous light, in a world where increasingly we are finding soul mates not necessarily in our denominational groupings but across them. Roman Catholic Canon law currently inhibits inter-communion, but in practice this often gives way to 'good conscience' custom as we find ourselves kneeling together with those whom we recognise as being in the fellowship of 'the Way' even though not in the structures of our denomination.

A New Way of Being Church

It was in the Roman Catholic Church that a new way of looking at the church and theological enquiry emerged in a Council, namelyVatican II, which met in the 1960s. What emerged from that Council made sense to many Anglicans, even while the Papacy itself ignored the results of Vatican II and was still modelling the reverse. Gregory Baum, a Canadian Jesuit priest, who was a 'peritus' (theological adviser) at the Council, prepared documents on religious liberty and ecumenism. He was also influential in writing the first draft of *Nostra aetate*, the Council document outlining a new look at the Roman Church's relationship with religions other than Christianity. Subsequently, going way beyond the Council's thinking, Baum developed his ideas in ways that have dovetailed with thinkers across the theological spectrum.

In his book *Faith and Doctrine* he sets out an understanding of what is called 'kenotic theology.'[7] This I have described (in Chapter 4) as imaging a God who is 'as weak as water, but as irresistible as a river'. Mission for Baum is no longer proclaiming a message which is 'the truth', about this God; rather, it is engaging with other people in a dialogue in which 'the Gospel note is sounded'; listening takes place all round, and, maybe, the 'inner eye of love is opened.' Such conversations should and must take place with people of all religions and none, and with those in differing Christian denominations. The purpose is not conversion, but 'a truly redemptive ministry', in which partners enter more deeply into a relationship through which they may discover the 'Naked God' in their lives, exploring and testing out what this means.[8] In order to be the church, the church needs the world, Baum says, because, in being 'aware' of that naked presence in the convictions and aspirations of others, we discover communion. In the 1980s Baum took this message to the Diocese of Quebec in Canada, developing 'convictions and aspirations' in a lively imaging of Christ's presence as 'church' with a Gospel for the poor manifest in its life and work. This I see as embodiment.

It was during the 1980s at an international conference in Germany (an outcome of CAACE – mentioned in an earlier chapter) that I came across this kind of thinking bubbling away beneath the surface in the Roman Catholic Church. One of the speakers was Father Andre Lascaris OP, then the Provincial (leader) of the Dominican Order in the Netherlands. His talk so interested me that I invited him to speak at the Department for Continuing Education in Oxford, on the 'hierarchical' model of Roman Catholicism, which he dismissed as a nineteenth-century invention, based on a false reading of the history of the medieval Church. Vatican II had tried to redress this, he said, but the present Pope (then John Paul II) for all his charisma, was reasserting a model from which we had to move on. Both Baum and Lascaris embraced subisidiarity (that is: decisions should be taken at the lowest possible grass roots level); advocated that dialogue must replace proclamation as a way of teaching; and suggested that embodiment must become the Church's way of life.[9] This sums up a very different way of being Church.

In 1997 the Anglican Bishop of Quebec, the Rt Rev. Bruce Stavert, invited me to lead a conference for his diocesan clergy with the title: 'Models for a Changing Church.' Under the heading 'Desiderata for Church Models' the programme was designed with these criteria and guidelines:

1. God spoken of and imaged in a way that can make sense to the un-churched.
2. Scripture interpreted, taking account of modern scholarship.
3. Liturgy resonating with the religious experience of twentieth-century culture as well as gems from history.
4. Educational process dialogic rather than didactic.
5. Open-ness to the experience and practice of other denominations and other religions.
6. Institutional forms, and shape of pastoral ministry to resonate with local needs and culture.

At the beginning of the clergy conference, I did a great deal of listening to become attuned to the French Canadian culture, while hearing the clergy's perception of the pastoral needs of their diverse congregations. Liturgy in French was new to me; the Eucharist from the *Book of Common Prayer* in French an eye opener. Pastoral ministry for many involved piloting an aeroplane to small scattered congregations. Openness to other denominations at the academic level was warm, but at local level resonated with old hostilities. As I discovered, even getting a postage stamp, let alone sharing a theological insight, was dangerous unless the conversation was in French.

This grid was offered as a basis for discussion throughout the conference, and it is offered here in case it is useful to readers.[10]

	Traditional	**Liberal**	**Radical**
Time	A cyclical pattern in which origins are important	Evolutionary and progressive	Past, present, and future interact dynamically leading to transfiguration
Society	Conceived as organic (e.g. feudal)	Conceived as pluralistic; the parts have a life of their own	Society is inter-dependent and each part is significant in its own right

Metaphor	Body controlled by head	Machine where an elite is needed to organise the parts	Collage – an artistic metaphor where power is given through participation
Power	Authority is mediated through a hierarchy	Power is about management	All contribute through participation and challenge
Challenge	Challenge is seen as deviant	Challenge has to be 'managed'	Challenge is necessary for creative growth
Ideology	Divine right: it is all ordained	The market leads	Conflict must be recognized and worked at

Ten years later it was another Roman Catholic scholar who clarified what was exciting many Anglicans. Gerard Mannion was Professor of Ecclesiology and Ethics at Liverpool Hope University. His book *Ecclesiology and Postmodernity* sets out his thinking. He sees the Roman Catholic Church since Vatican II torn between different factions, and without a clear vision. He does not deal with specific controversies, but rather sets out what that vision might be. He emphasises what many of us had already experienced, that 'one can often have more in common with a group of Christians from another denomination than with many in one's own Christian denomination. The lines of division among Christians are now transdenominational rather than interdenominational.'[11]

Mannion then sets out what he recognises as problematic in the Roman Catholic Church, and sees in all other Christian denominations to a greater or lesser extent.The list may be summarised as follows:

- voices of dissent against authority must be put down
- traditional doctrines and hierarchies must be adhered to
- prophecy (imagining a different future) is regarded with suspicion
- Catechesis (what is believed and taught) is instruction.

Both in the structure of the organisation and in its proclamation of the message, Mannion sees the Roman Catholic Church trying to restore a top down model of Church following the immediate euphoria of Vatican II, which in turn has led to disorientation and mixed messages. It involves repeated affirmation that the Holy See is the top of a hierarchy and holds the teaching authority.

Mannion's vision was that the relationship between the Church Universal and the Church Local should be turned upside down; that the local should lead and feed to the top, and the Pope should really be 'the servant of the servants of Christ' – an ancient Papal title, dating from the sixth century. Maybe its fulfillment has had to wait until the papacy of Pope Francis? Having a Pope (a Jesuit) who thinks along these lines has made both

Mannion's critique and his vision starkly visible in the life and politics of the Roman Catholic Church. What Francis models in his life, he is also attempting to inject into the institutional life of the massive Roman Catholic Church. This has attracted global attention and interest. However, as I write, the energetic but elderly Pope is faced by the institutional opposition that Mannion summarised, often expressed (because he is the Pope after all) in seemingly respectful requests for 'clarification' of his statements and aspirations, in the hope that these will then die the death of a thousand cuts.

Should the Pope's supporters gain the ascendancy, we should not expect a similar (or even a speedy) deconstruction of the Roman Catholic hierarchical model. For example, the Pope has flagged the exploration of having women deacons. Is this the first step towards the ordination of women? I don't think so. In England the process took about forty years from the first female deacons to the consecration of the first Church of England woman bishop. The Roman Catholic Church tends to work in centuries rather than decades, and there are certain barriers that cannot be crossed, the ordination of women being one. However, what we are seeing in Francis' exploration, may be a small step in a long haul towards women's place in the leadership of the Roman Catholic Church, in forms about which it is too early to speculate. There is no theological problem in having a woman cardinal for example, and in medieval times abbesses, though not ordained, sometimes wielded enormous authority. Hildegard of Bingen, a German

Benedictine Abbess of the twelfth century had great power both within and outside her Order, fighting ecclesial institutional corruption, and exploring poetry, song and drama in the liturgy. She was an intellectual polymath, and also a mystic in the sense discussed in chapter 4. Julian of Norwich, English and a century later, provides another example of one whose influence in articulating 'God talk' and prayer is still being uncovered.

Pope Francis' visit to Poland, in July 2016, to celebrate world youth day, brought 35,000 young pilgrims together and also showed how the Gospel can awaken them from the hidden persuaders of the media. 'Being here changes prejudices towards refugees and those who are different' said one Italian youngster. The Pope spoke of frustration, anger and violence and said 'You can't just be bitter and angry – our response has to be love, difficult though that may be.' He urged them to consider becoming politicians and social activists to ensure their faith would lead to concrete action.[12]

Hurry Up Please, it's Time

While the Roman Catholic church may need to take the long view, I am persuaded that the Church of England needs to act now, and that in doing so we shall serve the Kingdom, and indeed the wider church as it seeks to recover its role as an image of the Kingdom rather than a stumbling block.

So how does new God talk, church re-imagining and wrestling members affect the ordinary person in and out of the pew? In a rural village in a Church of England benefice (code for a collection of parishes) where the Rector is responsible for seven church buildings and has seven congregational structures to support, most members would listen with sympathy and some understanding to a sermon on the above; but when it gathers for a meeting about 'change' would be as resistant as any of Pope Francis' conservative cardinals, probably using similar techniques. Generous giving, caring pastoral work, outward looking initiatives, a few people investing much hard work in 'supporting the Rector', and a variety of liturgical experimentation, together with a friendly welcome and good use of the church building for concerts and other community happenings, gives it all a good feel, and is often effective, but does not perhaps grasp the need for restructuring for the duration.

In the 1980s in the Church of England, the movement towards team and group ministries, together with an influx of non-stipendiary ministers, was a factor in enabling ministry in (for example) rural Norfolk to manage the care of people, while radical measures were taken to de-commission churches, while conserving the heritage.[13] Today, in the Thames valley, for example, in spite of similar measures during that period, and the strengthening of lay education and ministry, there are still rural villages where one stipendiary priest, perhaps with a non-stipendiary minister or self-supporting minister, is serving seven or more parishes, each with a Parish

Church Council, an aging and diminishing congregation, and a resistance to change. We are still in danger of substituting 'I believe in holy and energetic clergy' for 'I believe in the Holy Catholic Church' as Herbert Kelly said in 1916 – a hundred years ago! What is needed (as Kelly also said) is the replacement of the whole system and the localisation of church life.

People's Church

In 2010, I was taken to a small downtown church in San Francisco for a mid-week Communion service. I walked into the Church of St Gregory of Nyssa and was confronted by a throng of people milling about the nave of the church which had been cleared of pews and was set up like a market place, groaning with food collected from a large food bank. The recession was biting and there were about 500 people – Chinese, Mexican, Caucasian and many other ethnicities – who relied on their visits to St Gregory's for subsistence.

But now many began gathering towards the worship space at the Chancel end of the building, which was prepared for the Communion. It was a chaotic service, with everyone who wished being given a part. I was handed a thurible with incense. 'What shall I do with it?' 'When you feel like it, cense anything, whether it moves or not.' was the reply. No one was 'vetted' because all, whether criminal, alcoholic, drug dependent or simply poor, were human. As team leader Sara Miles[14] said to

me afterwards, 'We aren't bound together by our same-
ness, or political views or cultural interest; we are bound
together by Christ's peace, which notably passes human
understanding.' During the communion, which was
distributed one to another, the priest disappeared and
then, after a blessing, re-appeared wearing an apron, with
volunteers bearing soup and bread and fruit, which was
shared around. Then the 'congregation', invited to take
what they needed, went into the nave with trolleys,
taking what they wished. No doubt some took advantage
– probably regularly – but no one was judging. What
impressed me most was that there was no 'them' and
'us', no 'clients' and 'middle class volunteers'; here were
human beings working at a task together.

Since that occasion, the pace of such local initiatives
has quickened to a torrent, in the USA, Europe and
the UK. Churches are being re-configured to provide
different versions of food banks, post offices, play groups,
cafes, and a host of other community facilities. Worship
is still central, but takes place within a community hub.
Of course some significant churches like St Martin-in-
the-Fields in London, have a decades old tradition and
practice of this kind, which in succeeding generations
it has developed and renewed. Now however, many
networks from inside the Church at large are resourcing
a variety of local initiatives of which the Church Urban
Fund (set up as a result of the controversial Faith in the
City report, as noted earlier) and Inclusive Church are
both excellent examples. These provide both theological
education as well as practical support.

A 'Trinity' Model to Pursue?

The Church Urban Fund is now sponsoring the mustard seed appeal, the network for making money-lending facilities available for the needy, which Archbishop Justin Welby pioneered in his publicised battle with pay day loan sharks in 2012 when he was Bishop of Durham. Two years later, as Archbishop of Canterbury, he launched a scheme for the Church of England to make available funds to set up credit unions, making facilities for people to save or borrow at reasonable cost, through the 16,000 parishes that serve the community in England. However, it was made clear that he hoped that these local initiatives would galvanise not just churchgoers, but many others in the community, caring compassionate people who are neither believing nor belonging, to join such an enterprise, and so it is proving. This provides a vibrant example of 'bottom up' ecclesiology: a perceived community need, 'top' sponsorship, with joint top/ bottom planning, energising and resourcing, followed by local provision. Let us call this a 'Trinity' model.

Another Church Urban Fund venture following a similar pattern is designed to meet the needs of the lonely and socially isolated. Launched in August 2016 the Full Community Sponsorship Scheme, was designed to make a contribution to the continuing global flow of refugees by providing a welcome for them in the UK. That this is a 'crisis' is an acknowledged grass roots concern polarising opinion; increasing intolerance among those who feel threatened; generating anxiety in those who find a conflict between head and heart, and at the same time fuelling among some a fervent outgoing compassionate urge to be involved in welcoming refugees who have lost everything. This scheme also follows the Trinity model, being launched jointly by the Archbishop of Canterbury and Amber Rudd, the British Home Secretary, on the basis of the perceived need, and the Government promise to receive direct from Syria 20,000 refugees. They will of course be vetted before being allowed into the UK. Then registered charities, or community groups of congregations or businesses will be able to sponsor families in collaboration with the local authority in which the sponsorship is situated. The sponsors will then be responsible for a continuing welcoming and settlement programme for the refugees they accept, offering accommodation, language skills, cultural integration of all sorts – and friendship. The Archbishop has welcomed such a family from Syria into the Lambeth Palace complex where he lives.

The Trinity model is being extended to parishes, ensuring that community needs are on the agenda. A Parish Church Council (PCC) with its lay representatives, together with the clergy, formulate a plan, offering it to the Bishop (and, as an aside, we might say that bishops need to be more local) or to priests like the Roman Catholic 'episcopal vicars', for scrutiny, resourcing and local oversight, then the plan will go back to the parishioners and local partners for implementation. Current progress in such models builds on the work of the former Archbishop of Canterbury, Rowan Williams, for whom inter-faith understanding and collaboration was and (remains) a major priority. His ability to form warm relationships with his Christian ecumenical partners, including Cardinal Murphy O'Connor, his successor Cardinal Vincent Nicholls, and all heading up the 'Christians Together' network, provided a firm basis for the various inter-faith forums with Muslims, Jews, Hindus, and Sikhs, together with their networks that have become integrated into the way of life for large numbers of faith community leaders. In 2010, while still Archbishop, Williams took up the then Prime Minister's (rather vague) concept of 'The Big Society' and gave it teeth by adopting the 'Trinity' model with his inter-faith colleagues, collaborating with the Community Ministers in how to increase and resource the already considerable numbers of faith-based volunteers in areas needed to help the poor, marginalised, elderly and vulnerable in a society hit by economic recession.

Regardless of falling numbers, the place of the Church of England, by law established in England (not the rest of the UK) has had some acknowledged advantages for faith leaders; although what that now really means, and what the future holds, needs careful consideration and debate.

The work of transformation has been widely spread, among voluntary bodies of various kinds. Marcus Braybrooke, a Anglican priest, is Joint Chair of the World Congress of Faiths, and Co-founder of the three faiths Forum. Like me, he has worked with Kamran Mofid's 'Common Good initiative'. The work and presence of the Islamic Centre in association with Oxford University has offered a stimulating opportunity to offer educational and inter-faith opportunities throughout the university, and for many years in association with the Department for Continuing Education. I have been impressed by and involved with the work of the Graduate Theological Foundation in the USA, changing from a Christian Education Institute to a multi-faith one. Readers may have had other and different experiences, or out on the streets have witnessed the follow up after an 'incident,' when volunteers from all faiths have turned out together to assist in the clean up, or mourn together in mutual respect and grief for death and injury.

Learning to Nourish the Human Spirit

Before closing this chapter on the church, we should have a word about how we train clergy for the future. As the pattern of social and cultural life in England has changed, so the church has responded with variations to its investment in training for clergy and lay members, and more recently, wrestlers.

The number of residential colleges diminished after 1965, and those remaining gradually became more open, associated with rigorous and varied degree opportunities and a changing curriculum. The non-residential courses of the 1980s and 1990s were of varying quality and, certainly, in the area I know well, it was a good move when the Oxford course, after flourishing for a decade in a link with St Alban's diocese, in the new century found a home at Ripon College, Cuddesdon. There, under the principalship of Martyn Percy, the Oxford course diversified its curriculum, revitalised its spiritual heart, and included opportunities for a wide variety of seekers in the new culture that was emerging.

Sarum College in Salisbury Cathedral Close (formerly Salisbury Theological College, which was closed in the early 1990s) was also developed for the new age by its second Principal, Keith Lamdin, and now, under the leadership of James Woodward, has a collection of 'Centres' for learning.[15] It has university-linked programmes as well as many that are not. The Centres include not only those with a new take on basic theological and spiritual disciplines but also, for example, one entitled the 'Centre for Theology, Imagination and Culture'. I am hopeful there are many more examples of innovative change in recruitment, content, style of learning and pastoral guidance emerging, and that a rich pattern may emerge up and down the country as the Church of England engages with the changes that are upon us.

Last Chance Saloon?

If you had difficulty in recalling the film *Life of Brian* then maybe the 1895 Punch cartoon of 'The Curate's Egg' will present even more difficulty. A fresh faced curate is being presented with a bad egg but, wishing to please, remarks 'It is good in parts.' The fact that the Church and other Faith networks, at national and local level, are living differently and serving imaginatively is good and encouraging; but it is only good 'in parts'. We are still faced with cultural disorientation, and our renewal is scattered and chaotic. Chaos does not necessarily lead to creativity, but it can help us to see what is important, and what is disposable. I believe the Woolf Report is right when it points to the need for a kind of Magna Carta, recognised by all, a statement of principles and values that foster the common good, and underpin our public life. We need to reflect on how this may be achieved, what may inhibit it, and what preparations we need to make to ensure that the good practice all around us, the experienced leaders who are pioneers, and the development projects that are still embryonic, are coordinated at least at regional level.

Meanwhile, in the scale of a lifetime, the 'Anglican Agony' of the past quarter of a century may come to be seen as a prophetic forerunner of change with the Church of England – as a kind of John the Baptist who prepares 'the Way'. The crisis of the Church of England with its diminishing congregations, lack of 'rapport' with at least three generations and another on the way, is real. 'Vincent' said a friend to whom I tried to explain this, 'You've lost your head.' 'Well yes, but so did John the Baptist didn't he?' I replied. However, this is not a death wish. Unlike some, perhaps many, of my fellow wrestlers, I have loved the Church of England with its history and its idiosyncrasies, and there are things about it I cherish and which I think need to flourish beyond the response to the crisis. Preparations for all these things will be needed, because the bridges to achieve them are shaky and the barriers are many. These bridges and barriers are considered in the next chapter, the Postlude to the book.

POSTLUDE

Barriers and Bridges

The Ram's Horn

'When you hear the blast of the rams' horns
you shall raise a great shout,
and the walls of the city will collapse.'[1]

In the mythic tale told in the Jewish Scriptures, we have
a typical religious tribal conflict, but in the unfolding of
the story and the sounding of the rams' horns, there is an
opportunity to introduce this Postlude. In this story, the
preparations that preceded the operation were complex,
and involved people with multiple identities, godly and
ungodly. The lesson is that barriers will only fall after
much active preparation and collaboration, and that is
what this chapter is about.

Mine has been a very small corner of the global picture,
but the glow of candles round about has illuminated a
wider scene, and has helped the wrestlers in search of
identity – with different outcomes. I am conscious of much

personal failure, but have picked up the glimmerings of 'something more' as others have lit up the scenery. These glimmerings I have tried to pursue. I cannot pretend to a 'Merton' experience, yet when the horrendous Paris attack on the newspaper was carried out a few years ago, I found myself saying 'Je suis Charlie' with deep feeling, but also (confusingly) 'Je suis Mohammed' in solidarity with the majority of Muslims, who are not terrorists, but were distressed by the *Charlie Hebdo* magazine's attacks on their beliefs. 'Will someone tell me who I am?' cries King Lear as events beyond his control crowd in on him; and for myself I know that it is only in the company of the Eucharistic fellowship of those who follow 'the Way' that I can repeatedly ask that question and hope eventually to be enlightened by pursuing it in that company.

Rowan Williams in his Dimbleby Lectures 'Nations, Markets and Morals', in 2002, speaks of our 'multiple identities' in twenty-first-century society. We may be a Muslim, Christian, Jew or Hindu, holding a job, supporting a football team or being a neighbour (different identities), but all with a religious affiliation seeing our lives as part of a larger story, giving an overall identity, which with its vision integrates and makes sense of each.[2] Lucy Winkett, Rector of St James's Piccadilly in London, makes an important addition to these multiple identities when she identifies our failure as human beings to live up to the vision, personally and corporately, with a gap between the compassion of our vision and action in our daily lives. We are for example, 'acutely aware of the suffering of the world, but also convicted of our own complicity in it.' While sometimes we are victims or in our best moments helpers, more often we are bystanders, or even perpetrators. Our identities in this respect are not fixed, and we are always in danger of hypocrisy. Yes, we have this 'solidarity'; but she identifies it as 'the solidarity of the shaken'.[3] The poet W. H. Auden tells us: 'You shall love your crooked neighbour, with your crooked heart.'[4]

However, knowing it is the solidarity of the shaken, many of us have found our solidarity in the Church of England, with all its deficiencies. I have called myself an 'outsider' but my long association as a wrestling but sometimes backsliding insider, makes me appreciative of the gracefulness and beauty of its liturgy, the stunning architecture of its buildings, and, so often, the self-sacrificial offering to the community of many among its congregations. If and when any of these disappeared it would be a tragic loss.

A medieval legend tells of the fallen angel who is asked 'What, in your exile from heaven, do you miss most?' 'The sound of the trumpets in the morning' is the reply.[5] That is nostalgia I suspect, and in our context something to be guarded against. While the Church of England is certainly not heaven, and many of my friends have experienced it as hell, there is nevertheless a whole collection of things belonging to the present institution of the Church of England that we must ensure will be there for future generations in our plural society. The presence and work of our great cathedrals is one, where worship and celebration of the arts, and presence in public life and public occasions is impressive. Sadiq

Khan, the new Muslim Mayor of London, elected to have his inauguration at Southwark Cathedral in 2016, a newly conceived event to add to the traditional historical remembrances and other public occasions that all cathedrals host, and will continue to host. Bishops in the House of Lords (alongside other faith leaders), is another, together with choral evensong (an innovation that the main author of the text, Archbishop Cramner, would not have dreamed of) in cathedrals, colleges and large parish churches up and down the land. Let us add bell ringing, a historical reminder of Christian presence daily, and in times of joy and sorrow. There are others, but my list will not help some wrestlers who are without my insider experience , and 'Je suis "Jacob" aussi'; so I need to change the anguished cry and yell from the inside 'Will someone tell *us* who we are?' The answer can only come from inside – us all.

So what do we need to do? We need to build bridges.

Building Bridges – Immersion

How do we resource the integration of the multiple identities within us: Jacob, Jacques, Mohammed and so on?

It is an old maxim that in order to experience another age, a different contemporary culture, an alternative way of thinking, or indeed another *identity*, we need to travel for a while in the shoes of those with whom we wish to identify. In his book *The Way of all the Earth*, John Dunne observes a phenomenon that he calls 'Passing Over'. In his version of wearing other shoes, he describes a *shifting of standpoint, moving to another culture, religion or life style.* He says the process is completed when one comes back, with the experience and insight of where one has been. He calls it 'the spiritual adventure of our time.'[6] It was while I was teaching with Ewert Cousins at a Graduate Theological Foundation Residential Institute that he introduced me to Dunne's thinking, and to his own experience as a young man of 'passing over' to a first nation people in the USA, and how it had changed him. It set me thinking about the importance of attitudinal change, and how one might offer a model of 'passing over'. Clearly, the best way is personal experience, an immersion such as Cousins had with his year-long embedded time in a Native American community. Some 'gap year' students doing voluntary service overseas, building schools, digging wells, teaching or providing some other simple support work in another culture, have the opportunity to experience at least a taster of this. But it is not practical for everybody.

Building Bridges – Shoes and Life Jackets

In the early part of the new century, in response to a request from 'Smithsonian Associates' to lead a seminar at Chatauqua in New York State, I devised 'The shoe-shop game'. Adult learning games involving role play make some of us impatient, like giving theological students 'tasters' of a life outside their experience, but both can contrive to link emotion to reason and open the mind. It is, after all, only a participative form of story telling, a kind of colloquium, and there are different ways of doing it. At Chatauqua in 2004, we arrived during the time when there was a passionate debate about what should be done at the site of 9/11. Some people present had personal involvement with the tragic event and its aftermath, and feelings were very strong. Working in threes (two people with opposing views and a monitor), a view was expressed and listened to by the 'other'; who then was invited to express the same view with equal accuracy and passion – in other words, to wear the other person's shoes. Choice of words, facial expression, body language and outward evidence of emotion, all played a part as roles were swapped, insights shared and evaluations were made. It was the kind of role-play that could only be done in a residential setting, with careful attention to social bonding and the 'return to home base'. The feedback was unanimously positive. Views were not necessarily changed, but listening and understanding was enhanced.

A powerful example was offered by St James Church, Piccadilly, in the heart of London in December 2015. A capsized rubber dinghy made for about 15 people, used by a group of 62 refugees from Syria to reach the Greek island of Lesbos, was suspended above the nave for the Christmas season, in a display created by artist Arabella Dorman. Three life jackets – two adult and one child – suspended over the side towards the congregation, reminded those beneath that the Christmas story includes the flight of Joseph, Mary and the child Jesus to Egypt as refugees, and that wearing the life jacket is more vital to understanding that story than saying 'Aah' over a crib.

It is now possible (and for many of the young generations a much more natural thing) to engage in participative virtual story telling over the internet. At the time of writing, PokeStops is the new game and 'Pokemon Go' is the Church of England's digital media office's follow up, with a blog to share with churches on ways of using it. Developing this modern form of story telling is going to be increasingly vital; but a counter-cultural difference may be our need to imagine how to create for the gamesters a return from virtual to real, if we believe that we need boots on the ground, and not in space, to effect the common good.

Other People's Bridges: Being Aware

A danger with bridge building is that we are so focused on our own constructs that we do not see when someone the other side of the river is throwing a Bailey bridge from that other side. The terrorist activities of Daesh, and the increase in UK people's fear of being overwhelmed by refugees and other migrants, has widened the gap between long term natives and English and other European Muslims, largely because the media and others insist on identifying them by religion rather than nationality: 'So called Islamic State' insists the BBC, instead of Daesh or Arabs or Africans. The radicalisation of young Muslims is complex and often personal; but part of it is their perceived exclusion from the mainstream culture of the generation to which they belong, by attitudes they meet at school, in the street or supermarket. For example, an employee in a supermarket in Merseyside may speak with the right accent, support 'the Reds', but may find it difficult to arrange shifts that enable him or her to go to the Mosque on a Friday, or come to an arrangement where s/he doesn't have to sell alcohol. The law is too heavy handed to deal with such issues,[7] but in spite of the bridges being crossed by scholars, Imams and many ordinary Muslims, not least shopkeepers, the cultural barriers imposed by the 'Britain Isn't What it Was Yesterday' brigade (the laager mentality) seem to be getting stronger, and in turn alienation or radicalisation is bound to increase. This is not to say that religion has not been, and is not today, responsible for much hatred, violence and war. But care must be taken in distinguishing where it is, from where it is not.

In South Africa and the USA in the 1960s, I was able to experience a 'taster' of Apartheid in the one, and the idealism of the young, and the post-Selma march hostilities among others at first hand. In both I experienced the laager[8] mentality.

Because SSM members had worked in South Africa from the very early days, with both pastoral and educational responsibilities, we had students from South Africa (black, white and coloured) coming to Kelham as ordinands, so at second hand I was familiar with the situation through them and through contemporary colleagues who were working there. However, as the apartheid regime extended its grip on the country, limiting the education that non-whites were allowed, the Society withdrew from the system, rather than compromising with the regime. This was at the same time as changes were taking place in the way the college at Kelham was run, and also coincided with Basutoland preparing for independence under Chief Leabua Jonathan – who many thought would 'nationalise' the schools in that country, when the moment came. A great number of those schools were resourced through SSM from the priory at Teyateyaneng.

I was sent, first to South Africa and then to Basutoland, in the winter of 1964/5 on a diplomatic mission for my community, to explain what was happening to the College at Kelham to the South African brethren; and then to carry back to England what they were worried about there. By chance, I travelled into South Africa with Father Simeon Nqwame, a black priest returning home from the College at Mirfield. He briefed me on the need to separate when we left the plane – total separation of black from white in all public places of course – and that if we met in the street (amid laughter) he would have to lower his eyes and adopt a servile attitude. It was no joke, and of course I knew about it. But that is not the same as experiencing it.

While in Johannesburg, attending a three day conference of the Christian Institute of South Africa, I found myself in the midst of a remarkable group of white clergy of all denominations; wrestlers who were making a theological critique of the regime and attempting to draw up a programme of positive action to undermine both the philosophy and the practice of the regime. A significant figure in this, who had founded the Christian Institute in that fateful year 1963, and lead speaker at the conference, was Dr Beyers Naude,[9] a Dutch Reformed pastor and former Moderator (Head) of the Dutch Reformed Church in South Africa. By this time he had rejected apartheid, been thrown out of the Reformed Church, and shunned by his local congregation. We met in the gents loo, and I began to open up a conversation with him. He put his finger to his lips and beckoned, and we walked in the garden. 'We are being bugged by CID' he said, 'And I don't want you to get detained.' At this moment I sensed the laager. Literally making wagons into a square fence or barrier, keeping the perceived enemy outside; I felt 'the enemy.'[10] Having had this taster experience, I was appalled, but did not immediately ask myself 'Can I wear Boer boots and learn what makes them act like this?' I wish I had, but later I tried to put on Naude's boots and feel something of the pain he had undergone in the reality of his pilgrimage as he built a bridge to break out of the Afrikaner laager into a new future for his country and his people.

Building Bridges into the Future

Preparatory work has to be done, and we have hard work ahead. Laagers have to be identified and shoes tried on.

The same goes for those of, say, Islamic faith coming to our shores who may have to redefine themselves with a new collective identity and an ability for self affirmation in the European context. They will need understanding and help by historic long term Brits and we will not be able to do it if we have not tried on their shoes.

As we have seen in earlier chapters, our values today are not fixed, and with new actors on the scene, new groups and new customs, we are together in a process of transformation, and we shall make new alliances some of which embrace parts of secular culture while others will be counter-cultural to the secular values of the market economy. The Christian understanding of embodying the divine in showing mercy and compassion is complemented in the Qu'ran, where every chapter but one is prefaced with the words: 'In the name of God, the Lord of Compassion, the giver of Compassion'. In her book *Hospitality in Islam: Welcoming in God's Name* Mona Siddiqui argues that Christian and Muslim understandings of hospitality have the special quality that both believe that God is a generous God, and that 'we must give and be generous because that is how God is, and God's giving knows no limits.' She goes on 'I would contend that offering hospitality, especially to the stranger, as a way of imitating the divine, as well as being obedient to God, is embedded in the rich vocabulary of charity, generosity, mercy and compassion which permeates the entire Qu'ran.[11]

This deeply embedded value is shared in Judaism through the tzedakah, which demands faithful giving to the needy as a priority, and to the depth that ensures those receiving never have to ask again. Together the Abrahamic faiths bring this enrichment to those compassionate people without faith, who in their lives prioritise and exhibit selfless compassion to the stranger, the vulnerable, the refugee and all who are needy.

There will be areas where Christian values and the values of those of other faiths are opposed, for example in the case of same-sex marriage. Mona Siddiqui and many other scholars, together with Imams responsible for pastoral care, reject a blanket reading of sharia law, and recognise that change can, and should, happen. Pointing to the way in which the Muslim world has contextualised Islam in different cultures, adapting it to widely different social, political and economic situations, Michael Nazir Ali instances the history of radical reconstruction in sharia law, and also the principle of *maslaha,* where change may be guided by taking into account the common good.[12] Nevertheless, there will be times when we all, Jew, Christian, Muslim, Hindu, Buddhist or whatever, find ourselves appalled by what is being said and done by those who bear our religious identity. In a pluralist State, we may need to practise Hooker's 'Harmonious Dissimilitude', which can only become harmonious if we build on the local face-to-face sharing that was outlined in the previous chapter, seeking understanding together when we hear or face the violence that is part of human nature, both within religious institutions as well as outside them.

There are many radical bridge builders into the future growth in the Church of England, as there are in all the religions here. The Reverend Andrew Cain gained press notoriety because he was the first licensed clergyman to marry a same-sex partner instead of crossing the legal toll bridge of a non-sexual civil partnership. What the press did not feature in such bold type was his transformation of the church of St James, West Hampstead, from a beautiful (but largely empty) church into one that has become a hub in the life of the local community, with a Post Office at the west end, a café, a physical play area for families and children, a shop – and a host of activities providing employment, *a welcome for all, of any faith and none*, as well as a refuge for the vulnerable. The beauty of holiness, and of worship, is preserved at the (open) East end where both traditional Anglo-Catholic and other kinds of worship are offered. St James is one church in a huge project, which is the Diocese of London's 'Capital Vision 2020'. In the Diocese of Oxford a full time pioneering appointment has been made to explore a new strategy and alternative forms of mission for the rural church. The Revd Val Plumb is currently serving four rural deaneries to research their situation in context, reflect, and consult with the Area episcopal team to enable action in that place. It is expected this will serve as a model for other parts of the diocese, to combat resistance to change, and 'envision' a church better able to serve the local community.

My experience has been that visionary theology and practice have not become embedded enough to be sustained. Passionate charismatic leaders move on, or die, and the legacy remains fragmented or dissolves. Can Andrew Cain, for example, with his grass roots team, win over a coherent majority of informed wrestlers, to join in ensuring the longevity and continuing development of their project at St James, West Hampstead? Are there other churches in similar city environments, or in suburban or rural contexts, willing to free their institutions from the tyranny of non-essentials, and look to the future with determination and imagination?

All institutions in the UK have lost the people's trust in recent years, including the Banks, the Stock Exchange, the Police, Trades Unions, Parliament and the Church. They no longer have authority. Can the Church of England, for example, stand out among these institutions and regain the idealism and enthusiasm of its lost generations in this atmosphere? I fear not, in a world drowning in the airwaves of Twitter, Facebook and the cynicism of journalists. It needs something new to do this. But 'I *am* doing a new thing' says the Lord. One of those Hebrew wrestlers called Isaiah picks up a recurring theme in the Jewish/Christian story: look around in the light of your story and respond to what is happening. Pope Francis has done this – responded – by opposing the 'free market' theory that assumes economic growth will 'trickle down' and benefit all.

> This opinion, which has never been confirmed by the facts, expresses a crude and naïve trust in the goodness of those wielding economic power

and in the sacralised workings of the prevailing economic system. Meanwhile the excluded are still waiting. To sustain a lifestyle which excludes others, or to sustain enthusiasm for that selfish ideal, a globalisation of indifference has developed. Almost without being aware of it, we end up being incapable of feeling compassion at the outcry of the poor, or weeping for other people's pain.[13]

Off With her Head

'Off with her head', said the Red Queen. 'Off...' 'Nonsense!'[14] said Alice, very loudly and decidedly, and the Queen was silent.

Anyone who lives, studies and teaches in the beautiful surroundings of Christ Church, Oxford, as Lewis Carroll did, knows a lot about the complexities of authority in institutions, in whatever century she/he is living. A lot of the rules governing church as institution need to be treated with Alice's bold reply, and this means imaginative liaisons – bridges of communication – between those suffering under 'nonsense' and the local bishop; and also at the next levels between bishop and archbishop; and between archbishop and government. In a story told in Luke's account (Luke 7:1–10) Jesus heals a slave belonging to a Roman Centurion; and he does so after a dialogue about the nature of authority beginning : 'I also am a man under authority'; not 'in authority' (Red

Queen speak) but under – the Greek word is 'hupo' – an authority which requires collaboration to work; being the word in action.

Has every Church of England diocese a 'Vision 2020' (or 2021/2022/2023), which is well publicised and working smoothly to eliminate nonsense and rescue the Christian presence in our communities? Only something as radical as this will capture the attention of the lost generations.

Kingdom Spotting for 'God's Spies'[15]

In the excellent recent book *Together for the Common Good*, the editors end their introduction by saying, 'The Common Good is that without which (call it, in concrete terms, family, community, city, nation, or the body of humanity itself), there can be no individual flourishing, and through which the individual discovers himself or herself anew: a person-in relation, unique, engaged, of infinite worth.'[16]

Since the publication of that book in 2013, the Woolf Report of the Commission on Religion and Public Life offers a checklist of next steps in its final chapter 'Ways Forward', and these steps come under the umbrella of 'a statement of the principles and values that foster the common good, and should underpin and guide public life'. For Christians, this will involve a really serious amount of 'Kingdom spotting'; that is, acknowledging and joining in all projects that are creatively nurturing the common good, whatever their source, and learning from each what has enabled good practice. For us, this is a realisation of Kingdom present, and our faith partners, who are doing the same, will learn our language and step into our shoes, while we learn from them what they call the process and step into theirs. There will need to be an effective coordinating body, and perhaps by 2017 this will be in place. It seems to me that it is this Commission that has sounded the Ram's Horns. We are in the business of creating a society in which we all, from our different religions, cultures, ethnic backgrounds and tribal self understanding, are able to feel at home, at ease with our difference and excited at the opportunities before us.

Is it possible? Can the Church become more Kingdom shaped?

Jesus proclaimed the Kingdom, but we got the Church, said the Roman Catholic Alfred Loisy in 1902 referring back to Christian beginnings.[17]

What about today? Can the church become more 'Kingdom shaped'?

I began with the enigmatic Herbert Kelly, so I shall end with him:

'There is what we intend to do, what we actually do, and what God makes of it.'

So let's proclaim the Kingdom, be aware of its embodied presence beyond our institutions and expectations, and build bridges of hope.

Upend the rain stick and what happens next
Is music you never would have known to listen for
In a cactus stalk.

Downpour, sluice-rush, spillage and backwash
Come flowing through. You stand there like a pipe
Being played by water, you shake it again lightly.

And diminuendo runs through all its scales
Like a gutter stopping trickling. And now here comes
A sprinkle of drops out of the freshened leaves.

The subtle little wet of grass and daisies,
Then glitter-drizzle, almost breaths of air.
Upend the stick again.
What happens next

Is undiminished for having happened once,
Twice, ten, a thousand times before
Who cares if all the most that transpires
Is the fall of grit or dry seed through a cactus.

You are like a rich man entering heaven
Through the ear of a raindrop.
Listen now again.

(Seamus Heaney, 'The Rain Stick')

Notes

Acknowledgements
1   George Every, *Poetry and Personal Responsibility* (London: SCM Press 1949) p. 95.

Prelude
1   *Living with Difference: Community, Diversity and the Common Good*, published by the Woolf Institute, Cambridge, December 2015.
2   Philip Bobbitt, *The Shield of Achilles - War, Peace, and the Course of History* (New York: Penguin, 2002) Bobbitt is a former Senior Director of Stategic Planning in both Democratic and Republican Administrations.
3   Ayn Rand and Nathaniel Brandon, *The Virtue of Selfishness* (New York: Signet, 1964)
4   A term coined by Colin Wilson who wrote a popular book with that title in 1956 about the search for meaning in human life through exploring the writings of a wide range of artists who felt at odds with society. See Colin Wilson, *The Outsider* (London: Gollancz, 1956).
5   Robin George Collingwood, *The Idea of History* (London: Oxford University Press, 1946) p. xii, as quoted by Edward Hallett Carr, *What is History?* (London: Macmillan, 1961) p. 30. Collingwood's original quotation came from a letter from Collingwood to the British Hegel scholar, T. M. Knox.

Chapter 1 The Naked God
1   Dietrich Bonhoeffer, *Who is Christ for Us?*, Craig L. Nessan and Renate Wind, eds (Minneapolis, MN: Fortress Press, 2002) p. 41.
2   Herbert Kelly, *The Gospel of God* (1929). (New edition with a memoir by George Every, SSM; London: SCM Press, 1959.)
3   Bonhoeffer, *Who is Christ for Us?* p. 79.
4   John Macquarrie, *On Being a Theologian: reflections at eighty* (London: SCM Press, 1999) p. 51.
5   See *An Interrupted Life: The Diaries and Letters of Etty Hillesum 1941-1943* (London: Persephone Books, 1999)
6   John Zizioulas, *Being as Communion: Studies in Personhood and the Church* (London: Darton, Longman and Todd, 1985) p. 17, 16. Zizioulas has taught at universities in Athens, Edinburgh and Glasgow, and is the Metropolitan of Pergamon.
7   Zizioulas, *Being as Communion* pp. 178-81.

8   Matthew 5:3–12; cf. Luke 6:20–22.

Chapter 2 Clothed in Flesh
1   Survey carried out with You-Gov Fieldwork, December 2015. By 2016 the number of Nones was 46% and rising. See a summary of the findings at: http://www.lancaster.ac.uk/news/articles/2016/why-no-religion-is-the-new-religion/
2   Geza Vermes (1924–2013) was Professor of Jewish Studies in the University of Oxford. Born to Jewish parents, adopted by Roman Catholics during the holocaust, he became a Roman Catholic priest and worked on the Dead Sea Scrolls. Later he returned to the Judaism of his birth, and produced a series of books on the Jesus of history, beginning with *Jesus the Jew* (1973).
3   *Daily Telegraph* 18 April 2005. For his development of these ideas, see his book *Christian Beginnings: From Nazareth to Nicaea* (New Haven and London: Yale University Press, 2012)
4   The language of commerce, and also of the text of Jewish Scriptures published in BCE 275, which much later became the basis for the Christian version of the Bible.
5   A phrase said to have been used by a former scholar-bishop of Durham, David Jenkins (1925–2016) in the 1980s. He really said that the resurrection is real, but not a literal physical event ('a conjuring trick with bones').
6   Teresa Morgan, *Roman Faith and Christian Faith* (Oxford: Oxford University Press, 2016) p. 154. Teresa Morgan is Fellow of Oriel College, Oxford, and Professor of Graeco-Roman history at Oxford University, and an Anglican priest.
7   Henry Chadwick, *Tradition and Exploration* (Norwich: Canterbury Press, 1994) p. 270
8   See N. T. Wright, Keith Ward and Brian Hebblethwaite, *The Changing Face of God: Lincoln Lectures in Theology 1996* (Lincoln: Lincoln Cathedral Publications, 1996) pp. 30–41.
9   Richard Hooker, *Of the Laws of Ecclesiastical Polity* Book V.liv.6.
10   The anthropologist Robert Randulph Marrett recommended the word to Murray. For more on this word and Murray's inclusion of it in the OED, see Sarah Ogilvie, *Words of the World. A Global History of the Oxford English Dictionary* (Cambridge: Cambridge University Press, 2013) p. 95.
11   Karl Rahner, *Foundations of the Christian Faith: An Introduction to the Idea of Christianity* (1978). He says that *every* person is ordained to communion with God.
12   Jane Shaw, 'Cultivating a Moral Imagination: Religion, Art and Humanities in the Public Sphere'. Vincent Strudwick Lecture, Kellogg College, Oxford, 2012.
13   In his *Hope Without Optimism* (New Haven and London: Yale University Press, 2015) Terry Eagleton makes the suggestion that hope is more a disposition than a cognitive or emotional state.
14   A phrase used by the writer of the letter to the Hebrews, Chapter 10 verse 20.
15   George Every (1909–2003) was an historian, theologian, writer on Christian mythology and poet. He was a member of SSM until 1970 when he became a Roman Catholic and thereafter taught at Oscott, where he assisted in the library, did some teaching and continued to research and write. His *Byzantine Patriarchate* (1947) (London: SPCK, 1962, revised edition) marked his continuing interest in Eastern Christianity, and his *Christian Mythology* (London: Hamlyn, 1970) develops some of Christopher Dawson's work. His *Poetry and*

Responsbility (London: SCM Press, 1949) provoked a sparky debate with F.R. Leavis on the distinction between a Christian poet and a poet who happens to be a Christian. He contributed to the Symposium celebrating T.S. Eliot's 60th birthday with an essay titled 'The Way of Rejections' in *T.S. Eliot: A Symposium*, R. March and Tambimuttu, eds (London: Tambimuttu & Mass, 1948), pp. 181-8.

16   William Temple, *Nature, Man, and God* (London: Macmillan, 1934) pp. 318, 315.

17   Herbert Kelly, 'Ad Fratres', privately circulated to the members of SSM in 1906

18   Selections from Dawson's works, including this essay, are in *Christianity and European Culture: Selections from the work of Christopher Dawson,* Gerald J. Russello, ed. (The Catholic University Press of America, 1998) pp. 34.

19   Dawson in Russello, *Christianity and European Culture*, p. 35 A similar thesis has been put forward recently by Professor Andrew Walls of Edinburgh.

20   Diarmaid MacCulloch, *Silence in the History of the Church* (London and New York: Penguin, 2011).

21   Dawson, 'The Judgement of the Nations' in Russello, *Christianity and European Culture* p.190.

22   I am indebted to the late Professor John Dunne of the University of Notre Dame for this insight

23   'Prayer to the Holy Ghost' in *Seasons of the Spirit*, George Every, Richard Harries and Kallistos Ware, eds (London: SPCK, 1984) p.166.

Chapter 3 Frozen Assets

1   Canon John Fenton DD (1921-2008) was a Canon of Christ Church from 1978-91 and a provocative teacher of the New Testament to generations of students. He likened New Testament studies to working with an old painting and removing all the later accretions. Among his books, his study of St Matthew's Gospel (London: Pelican, 1963) illustrates his scholarship and approach.

2   Roland Walls (1918-2011) was a novice in SSM (and gave me some tutorials there). He was a Cambridge don, then founder of the Community of the Transfiguration. See Ron Ferguson, *Mole Under the Fence* (Norwich: Hymns Ancient and Modern, 2006) and John Miller, *A Simple Life: Roland Walls and the Community of the Transfiguration* (Norwich: St Andrew Press, 2014) for an insight into this extraordinary theologian and wonderful human being.

3   Dennis Nineham was Regius Professor of Divinity at Cambridge, Warden of Keble College Oxford, and head of the Church of England doctrinal Commission. Dennis Nineham, *Saint Mark* (Philadelphia: Westminster Press, 1963) and *The Use and Abuse of the Bible: A Study of the Bible in an Age of Rapid Change* (New York and London: Macmillan, 1976).

4   For example: If a poor man comes to the Eucharist late the bishop, not the deacon, greets him and offers him his seat.

5   On this discovery, see Janet Martin Soskice, *Sisters of Sinai: How Two Lady Adventurers Found the Hidden Gospels* (London: Chatto & Windus, 2009)

6   Tertullian c.155-c. 240 CE was a prolific author writing in Latin from the Roman province of Carthage in Northern Africa. He was a significant figure in bringing order and cohesion to the variety of understanding of what Christians believed and stood for. This passage comes as an aside, in his attack on Marcion, another early leader. *Adv Marcion* III, xiii

7   I owe this thought to the late Sir Timothy Raison, statesman and man of letters, whose exhibition of artistic works relating to the Magi was presented in 1995/96.

See *We Three Kings - The Magi in Art and Legend* (Aylesbury: Hazell Books, 1995).

8   Dawson, 'The Classical Tradition and Christianity' in Russello, *Christianity and European Culture*, p.157

9   Augustine of Hippo (b. 354) was one of the pre-eminent theologians of the West, whose conversion to Christianity is told in remarkable detail in his *Confessions*. He became Bishop of Hippo in 395 and remained in that position until his death in 430.

10 Thomas More (1498-1535) was a lawyer and social philosopher, and the Chancellor of England (1529-32) to Henry VIII. He could not accept the separation from the Roman Catholic Church that Henry VIII inaugurated and was subsequently executed.

11 Conventional shorthand for Geneva (Protestantism) and Rome (Catholicism).

12 Richard Hooker, *Of the Laws of Ecclesiastical Polity* (hereafter *Laws*); all quotations are from an edition of the Oxford University Press printed MDCCCL, based on the Keble edition of 1836. *Laws* 1 xvi.8

13 *Laws* I.

14 *Laws* III.xi.9.

15 *Laws* V.liv.5

Chapter 4 Open to the Spirit?

1   'Theoria' is a conviction of something 'seen' to be true, which then needs testing out by formulating a theory.

2   Commissioned by Fr Stephen Bedale SSM who had seen Jagger's Artillery Memorial in Hyde Park. It was in place for the opening of the Chapel in 1928.

3   Alister Hardy (1896-1985) was Professor of Zoology at Oxford, a Darwinian marine biologist and Templeton prize-winner who founded the Religious Experience and Research Unit in 1969. That research unit is still active, and from 2000 has been located at the University of Wales, Lampeter.

4   *Living the Questions* ed. with an introduction by Edward Robinson (Oxford: Manchester, College, 1978)

5   See Thomas Merton, *The Seven Storey Mountain* (1948); *The Sign of Jonas* (1953); and *Bread in the Wilderness* (1953).

6   Thomas Merton, *Conjectures of a Guilty Bystander* (London: Penguin, 1968) p. 140

7   In his poem, 'Hurrahing for Harvest.'

8   Ralph Martin, *Towards a New Day - a Monk's Story* (London: Darton, Longman and Todd, 2015)

9   John Moses, *Divine Discontent: the prophetic voice of Thomas Merton* (London: Bloomsbury, 2014) p. 206

10 Moses, *Divine Discontent* p. 207

11 Gerard Manley Hopkins, *Poems and Prose* selected and ed. W. W. Gardner (London: Penguin 1953) Hopkins (1844-89) was a Roman Catholic convert from Anglicanism; a Jesuit and poet.

12 A phrase coined by Jane Shaw to describe the direct apprehension of, and the communication people have, with God, in her Eric Symes Abbot Memorial Lecture at Westminster Abbey and Keble College Oxford, entitled *The Mystical Turn*, May 2008.

13 Personal correspondence with Dame Felicitas Corrigan (1908–2003), who was a scholar and writer, as well as spiritual mentor to many, including Siegfried Sassoon and Alec Guinness.

14 Ephesians 3:17–19.

15 Jurgen Habermas, *An Awareness of What is Missing: Faith and Reason in a Post Secular Age* (London: Polity Press, 2010). Habermas is Professor of Philosophy Emeritus at the University of Frankfurt.

16 Margaret Masterman, philosopher and authority on linguistics, was married to Richard Braithwaite, sometime Knightsbridge Professor of Moral Philosophy at Cambridge. Dorothy Emmet was Professor of Philosophy at Manchester University. They were the founding members of the Epiphany Philosophers. Rowan Williams joined the group later.

17 In George Herbert's poem 'Prayer' which is a deeply complex, beautiful meditation on practice, he speaks of prayer in a collation of images as a 'kind of tune'; which I think Every had in mind.

18 Dietrich Bonhoeffer, *Letters and Papers from Prison* (New York: Macmillan, 1953), p. 237

19 Carlo Rovelli, *Seven Brief Lessons on Physics*, translated by Simon Carnell and Erica Segre (London: Penguin Allen Lane, 2015) pp. 74–5.

20 In an '*Alice in Wonderland*' sermon the Revd Anne Kiggel speaks of the Pentecostal moment 'fading fast to the faintest memory of a vanishing smile'.

21 John Zizioulas, *Being as Communion* (Crestwood, New York: St. Vladimir's Seminary Press, 1997) p. 17.

22 Imaginative work on pilgrimage and the opening up of many ancient paths in UK, can be accessed by BritishPilgrimage.org. The website describes them as 'Making journeys to holy places. Bring your own beliefs…'

23 *An Interrupted Life: The Diaries and Letters of Etty Hillesum 1941–1943* (London: Persephone Books, 1999) p. 229.

24 This is taken from a conversation between Ivon Hitchens and my wife, Nina, also an artist, who did a study of him while at College. In the 1970s we lived near him and his wife, and became friends. See also Alan Bowness, *The Development of Ivon Hitchens' Painting* (London: Lund Humphries, 1973) p. 32.

25 Wassily Kandinsky, *Concerning the Spiritual in Art* trans. Michael T.H. Sadler (London: Tate Publishing, 2006) p. 16.

26 John Taylor was in Africa as a teacher and researcher, became Secretary of the Church Missionary Society, then Bishop of Winchester. His books include *The Primal Vision* (1965) and *The Go-Between God* (1972). This poem was published in *A Christmas Sequence and other Poems* (Oxford: Amate Press, 1989).

27 John Taylor, *The Go-Between God* (London: SCM Press, 1972) p. 26.

28 Praxis: a process whereby a theory is embodied.

Chapter 5 The End of an Era

1 The essayists included Frederick Temple (later Archbishop of Canterbury) and Benjamin Jowett (later Master of Balliol College Oxford.) Their time was to come.

2 Subsidiarity is the process by which decisions are taken at most local level for those affected.

3 J.N. Figgis, *Churches in the Modern State* (New York and London: Longmans, Green and Co. 1913).

NOTES

4   The fledging SCM, which began in 1889, was a student missionary movement, and developed across national, cultural and denomination boundaries.

5   Both Temple and Kelly were deeply influenced by F. D. Maurice (1805–72), founder of Christian Socialism. Maurice was dismissed from his professorship at King's College, London for unorthodoxy, in the wake of his support of many new ideas expressed in his *Theological Essays* (1853). His other books included *The Kingdom of Christ* and *What is Revelation?* He was rehabilitated in academia, as Knightsbridge Professor at Cambridge in 1866, when the tide began to turn.

6   Herbert Kelly, *An Idea in the Working: an account of the Society of the Sacred Mission, its history and aims* (London: Mowbray, 1908) p. 27.

7   Herbert Kelly, 'Ad Filios' 1920/21 Published privately for students at Kelham pp. 9–10.

8   William Temple, *Christianity and Social Order* (1942) Ronald Preston, ed. (London: SPCK, 1976) p. 60.

9   William Temple, *Readings in St. John's Gospel. First series, chapters 1–XII* (London: Macmillan and Co., 1939) p. xxxi

10 William Temple, 'Presidential Address' to the WEA, October 21, 1911, printed in the WEA journal, *The Highway* December 1911.

11 Kelly, *An Idea in the Working*, p. 13.

12 See William Temple, *Christian Faith and Life* (London: SCM Press, 1931) (with four reprints that year).

13 T. S. Eliot, *The Idea of a Christian Society* (London: Faber & Faber, 1939). As noted earlier, Eliot first gave these lectures at Kelham. In the preface and elsewhere he acknowledged his debt to Christopher Dawson, and among others to Fr Gabriel Hebert SSM. However, it is not stated anywhere in print that he delivered the lectures first to the brethren and students at Kelham for a run-through. He acknowledges that George Every proof-read the final text for him; then notes that a 'distinguished theologian' (whom I judge to be George) made certain observations, which he quotes in full.

14 In *The Sense of an Ending* (Oxford: Oxford University Press, 1966) Frank Kermode calls Eliot a 'a poet of the apocalypse ... who prophesies the destruction of the earthly city as a chastisement of human presumption.' p. 112.

15 T. S. Eliot, *Christianity and Culture* (London: Harvest Books, 1977) p. 76.

16 C. S. Lewis sermon preached in the University Church, Oxford, 1939.

17 C. S. Lewis, *Weight of Glory* (New York: Harper Collins, 2001) p. 28.

18 William Temple, *The Hope of the New World* (London: Macmillan, 1940).

19 William Temple, *Personal Religion and the Life of Fellowship* (London: Longmans, Green and Co. 1926) pp. 2–3.

20 Richard Parsons ed., *Re-Educating Adults: an Essay in Adult Religious Education* (1945).

21 A convert to Roman Catholicism from Protestantism in 1939 (he had been a Lutheran minister), Louis Bouyer was a member of the 'Oratory' Religious Order and Professor at L'Institut Catholique de Paris. His books demonstrate his conviction that at the heart of Christianity was not doctrine or a particular liturgy, or customs and organisation, but the person of Jesus. He died in 2004.

22 Edna Mallett, 'Christian Penetration', SSM Magazine, March 1967.

23 I was its first Executive Secretary.

24 In 1985 The National Institute of Adult Continuing Education published jointly with CAACE a review of research and practice in adult education (by Alexandra

Withnall) and in the same year the first comprehensive review of education as a lifelong process appeared. I was asked to contribute an article entitled 'The Christian Churches in Adult Education'. See *Lifelong Education for Adults: An International Handbook* ed. Colin Titmus (Oxford: Pergamon Press, 1989).
25 See chapter 2.
26 Adolf Von Harnack, *What is Christianity?* (London: E. Benn, 5th edition, 1901) p. 13

Chapter 6 From Adaptionism to Radicalism
1   This is a point made in Andrew Brown and Linda Woodhead, *That Was the Church That Was* (London: Bloomsbury, 2016)
2   Timothy Raison (1929–2011) was a Conservative politician who had been Minister of State for Northern Ireland and, by the time of this report, was Minister for Overseas Development. I had first come across his name while I was at Kelham, when he had been founder and editor of *New Society* (1962) a forward looking journal of social change. In the 1960s he won the Nansen Refugee award for outstanding service to the cause of Refugees and Development.
3   One notable criticism of Runcie came in the traditional anonymous Preface to *Crockford's Clerical Directory*, which was always a short essay on the state of the Church of England. In December 1987, the author of that preface was The Revd Gary Bennett, Chaplain and Fellow of New College Oxford. Bennett took the opportunity to made a deep attack on the Archbishop for embracing secular liberalism. A combination of factors led to the sad suicide of the author soon after he was exposed as the Preface's author. The Preface was taken to be (and indeed it was) a comment on Runcie's leadership; but his strategy of attempting to encompass and manage the wide diversity of the Anglican Communion was in my view laudable. To the historian Bennett, it was a betrayal of his understanding of the Catholic heritage of the Church of England.
4   Anthony Russell, *The Clerical Profession* (London: SPCK, 1980). Russell was Bishop of Dorchester in the Diocese of Oxford from 1988 to 2000, and then Bishop of Ely from 2000 to 2010.
5   At this time the Anglican Communion had about 70 million members worldwide, with about 800 bishops.
6   Colin Craston ed., *Open to the Spirit – Anglicans and the Experience of Renewal* (London: Church House Publishing, 1987). Colin Craston was Vice Chair of Anglican Consultative Council – a sort of committtee with members from across the Communion. The twelve contributors included Grace Gitari, chairperson of the Mother's Union Diocese of Mount Kenya East; Winston Ndungane, later Archbishop of Cape Town; the Bishops of Singapore and South Central Brazil; the Archbishop of Sydney; Donald Allchin, Michael Harper, Frederick Borsch of Princeton University, Gordon Wakefield of the Queen's College Birmingham, and myself.
7   Craston, *Open to the Spirit*, pp. 5 and 6.
8   This is the John Taylor referred to in Chapter 4.
9   It reminded me of some lines from Robert Bolt's play about Sir Thomas More, *A Man for All Seasons* (1966), in the Introduction to Act 2: 'The Church of England, that finest flower of our Island, genius for compromise; that system peculiar to these shores which deflects the torrents of religious passion down the canals of moderation.' But of course the 'Universal' involved many ecumenical partners and

the Church the Communion included a majority from 'other shores'. Deflecting religious passions down the torrents of moderation wasn't going to be easy.

10 'Lambeth '98 Should Be "Less English"' *Church Times*, 18 November 1988, p. 1.

11 Richard Holloway was Bishop of Edinburgh from 1986 to 2000, and also Primus of the Scottish Episcopal Church from 1992 to 2000. His most recent brilliant book is *A Little History of Religion* (New Haven and London: Yale University Press, 2016). He tells his story in his memoir, *Leaving Alexandria* (Edinburgh: Canongate, 2012).

12 Vincent Strudwick, 'It's a Relationship, Not a Doctrinal Quiz' and Editorial 'Is the Communion Too Much Bother?' both in *Church Times*, 7 July 2006, p. 8

Chapter 7 Cosmic Transformation and Christian Responsibility

1 Slavica Jakelic is Assistant Professor of Humanities and Social Thought at Christ College at Valparaiso University. This quotation comes from a paper entitled 'Secularisation, European Identity and the "End of the West"'. Jakelic was speaking of tribal loyalties that negate the common good. I am using this quotation to indicate our belonging to the human race as moral agents, individually, and in the network of faith communities, as agents of the common good.

2 Seyyed Hossein Nasr, *Religion and the Order of Nature* (Oxford: Oxford University Press, 1996) p. 65

3 See Iris Origo, *The Merchant of Prato: Francesco di Marto Datini 1335-1410* (Nonpareil Books, 2002). R. H. Tawney, *Religion and the Rise of Capitalism* (1926) raised a significant debate on the subject. Tawney (1880-1962) was Professor of Economic History at the LSE and a leading Adult Educationalist, working with the WEA and University Extra Mural Departments.

4 Patrick Buchanan, *State of Emergency: The Third World Invasion and Conquest of America* (New York: St Martin's Press, 2006)

5 As quoted in A. Rashid, *Taliban: the Story of the Afghan Warlords* (London: Pan Books, 2001) p. 134.

6 Philip Bobbitt, *The Shield of Achilles: war, peace, and the course of history* (London: Anchor, 2002) p. 777.

7 As quoted by John Maitland, *Diverse Times, Sundry Places* (Brighton: Alpha Press, 1996) p. 114.

8 See 'Institut fur die Wissenschaften vom Menschen' Newsletter No 4: 86 (Autumn 2004).
   This Institute for Human Sciences, founded in 2000, publishes papers in English and other European languages.

9 See Matthew 19:24, Mark 10:24-27 and Luke 18:24-27.

10 Nicholas Sagovsky and Peter McGrail, eds, *Together for the Common Good: towards a national conversation* (London: SCM Press, 2015) p. 13. I prefer the word 'hope'; optimism may be an emotional state, but hope is disposition involving praxis.

11 There is a story in Luke 5:4 in which Jesus tells the disciples 'Launch out into the deep, and let down your nets for a draught.'

Chapter 8 Towards a Very Odd Church Indeed

1   John Taylor, 'The Future of Christianity' in John McManners ed., *The Oxford Illustrated History of Christianity* (Oxford: Oxford University Press, 2001) pp. 628–65.

2   Taylor quotes Vincent Donovan, *Christianity Rediscovered: An epistle from the Maasai* (New York: Orbis Books, 1982) p. 83.

3   Richard Holloway, *A Little History of Religion* (New Haven and London: Yale University Press, 2016) p. 189

4   See *Towards a Quaker View of Sex: an essay by a group of Friends* (London: Friends Home Service Committee, 1963) and the revised edition in 1964.

5   Ephesians 4:26.

6   Umberto Eco (1932–2016) Professor of Semiotics, and novelist. His books include the famous novel *The Name of the Rose*.

7   Gregory Baum, *Faith and Doctrine* (NY: Newman Press, 1969)

8   Baum, *Faith and Doctrine*, p.116

9   Baum's influence was behind the work of Professor Solange Lefebre who visited Kellogg College in 2009 and spoke on the Quebec Government's Commission dealing with religious freedom in that Province. Lascaris published in 2007, with three other Dominicans, a booklet *Church and Ministry* in which they advocated Gay relationships and Lay Celebration of the Eucharist.

10   The six points for making church and the grid were developed in some work I did with Alistair Redfern, then a tutor at Ripon College, Cuddesdon, later Bishop of Derby, to whom I am indebted.

11   Gerard Mannion, *Ecclesiology and Postmodernity: Questions for the Church in our Time* (Liturgical Press, 2007) p. 44.

12   Report in *The Tablet*, 6 August 2016 by Christopher Lamb.

13   For a discussion of this, see Vincent Strudwick, 'Local Ordained Ministry: Yesterday's Case for Tomorrow's Church' in *Theology*, May 1981.

14   See Sara Miles, *Jesus Freak – feeding, healing, raising the dead* (New York: Jossey-Bass, 2010)

15   Keith Lamdin is an Anglican priest and innovative theological trainer who worked in the Diocese of Oxford for many years, and pioneered the Centres and pattern of training that are now being built on.

Postlude Barriers and Bridges

1   In the mythic tale told in Joshua 5:15–6: 27 the walls of the city of Jericho will fall when the Rams' horns are sounded; it's a good story and the walls only fall after much active preparation, and collaboration with an interesting diversity of humanity, including Rahab the prostitute.

2   Rowan Williams, *Nations, Markets and Morals: The Richard Dimbleby Lecture*, 19 December 2002, available at http://rowanwilliams.archbishopofcanterbury.org/articles.php/1808/the-richard-dimbleby-lecture-2002

3   Lucy Winkett, *Blessed are the Hypocrites?* The 2016 Eric Abbott Memorial Lecture in Westminster Abbey and Keble College Oxford.

4   W.H. Auden, 'As I Walked Out One Evening' November 1937.

5   As recounted by Stuart Y. Blanch, *The Trumpet in the Morning* (Oxford: Oxford University Press, 1979) p. 3

6   John Dunne, *The Way of all the Earth: Experiments in Truth and Religion* (New York: Macmillan, 1972) p. ix.

7   'With customs we live well, but laws undo us.' So said the seventeenth-century poet, George Herbert (in his *Jacula Prudentum*).

8   The 'laager' was a way that Boer farmers protected themselves from attack by forming the wagons in a square so they were protected on all sides. It is a defensive position, almost always defeated by a persistent, well resourced siege. See chapter 8.

9   Colleen Ryan ed., *Beyers Naude: Pilgrimage of Faith* (Cape Town: Creda Press, 1990).
     At a meeting in New College, Oxford, I met and talked with Jane Mason who had collaborated with Colleen Ryan in gathering material for this book.

10   It was much later that Michael Lapsley SSM working as a university chaplain in South Africa was targeted by the regime's agents with a parcel bomb that left him semi-blind and without hands. He worked with Desmond Tutu in the post-Apartheid Truth and Reconciliation Commission and in 1998 founded the Institute for the Healing of Memories. See Michael Lapsley, with Stephen Karakashian, *Redeeming the Past: My Journey from Freedom Fighter to Healer* (Maryknoll, NY: Orbis Books, 2012)

11   Mona Siddiqui, *Hospitality and Islam* (New Haven and London: Yale University Press, 2015) pp. 124–5. Mona Siddiqui is Professor of Islamic and Interreligious Studies at the University of Glasgow.

12   Michael Nazir Ali, 'We Can Defeat Islamist Terror – But Not On Our Own,' in *Standpoint*, September 2016, Issue 85, p. 101.

13   From Pope Francis, *Evangelii Gaudium* (2013), quoted in Clifford Longley, 'Market Economics and Catholic Social Teaching' in *Together for the Common Good*, Sagovsky and McGrail, eds.

14   *Alice's Adventures in Wonderland* by Lewis Carroll; Chapter viii 'The Queen's Croquet-Ground.'

15   Lear to his daughter Cordelia, William Shakespeare, *King Lear*, Act 5, Scene 3: 'We'll think about the mysteries of God's universe as if we were God's spies.'

16   Nicholas Sagovsky and Peter McGrail, *Together for the Common Good: towards a national conversation* (London: Hymns Ancient and Modern, 2015) p. xxx.

17   Alfred Loisy (1897–1940) was a Roman Catholic priest, biblical scholar, and philosopher of religion. He held that the gospel and church should be subjected to the critical method if their real nature and purpose were to be understood. His *Gospel and the Church* (1902) was edited and re-issued in 1988 by Prometheus Books (New York). In the light of my earlier chapters, *La Naissance du Christianism* first published in 1948 by Allen and Unwin may also be useful.

Select Bibliography

This bibliography shows some of the reading that has informed and shaped the ideas in this text. In addition to the specific references in the endnotes, the titles may offer some more detailed follow up for wrestlers who are curious.

Augustine, *Confessions* **Chadwick, Henry, Trans.,** (Oxford: Oxford University Press, 1991)

Baum, Gregory, *Faith and Doctrine* (Michigan: Newman Press, 1969)
Biggar, N. and Hogan, L., *Religious Voices in Public Places* (Oxford: Oxford University Press, 2009)
Blanch, Stuart, Y., *The Trumpet in the Morning* (Oxford: Oxford University Press, 1979)
Bobbitt, Philip, *The Shield of Achilles: War, Peace and the Course of History* (Harmondsworth: Penguin, 2002)
Bonhoeffer, Dietrich, *Letters and Papers from Prison* (London: Macmillan, 1953)
Bonhoeffer, Dietrich, *The Cost of Discipleship* (London: SCM Press, 1959)
Bonhoeffer, Dietrich, Plant, Stephen and Burrows-Cromwell, eds, *Letters to London* (London: SPCK, 2013)
Bosanquet, Mary, *The Life and Death of Dietrich Bonhoeffer* (London: Hodder and Stoughton, 1968)
Botton, Alain, de, *Religion for Atheists* (Harmondsworth: Penguin, 2013)
Bowness, Alan, *The Development of Ivon Hitchens' Painting* (London: Lund Humphries, 1973)
Brown, A. and Woodhead, L., *That Was The Church That Was* (London: Bloomsbury, 2016)
Brydon, Michael, *The Evolving Reputation of Richard Hooker:An Examination of Responses 1600-1714* (Oxford: Oxford University Press, 2004)

Buchanan, Patrick, *State of Emergency: The Third World Invasion and Conquest of America* (New York: St Martin's Press, 2006)

Carr, Edward, Hallett, *What is History?* (London: Macmillan, 1961)
Chadwick, Henry, *Tradition and Exploration* (Norwich: Canterbury Press, 1994)
Chambers Dictionary of Beliefs and Religions (London: Chambers, 1992)
Colleen, Ryan, ed., *Beyers Naude: Pilgrimage of Faith* (Cape Town: Creda Press, 1990)
Collingwood, Robin George, *The Idea of History* (Oxford: Oxford University Press, 1946)
Cousins, Ewert, *A Spiritual Journey into the Future* (Wyndham Hall Press, 2010)
Craston, Colin, ed., *Open to the Spirit* (London: Church House Publishing, 1987)

Dawkins, Richard, *Climbing Mount Improbable* (Harmondsworth: Penguin, 1996)
Dawson, Christopher, *Progress & Society: An Historical Inquiry* (New York: Sheed and Ward, 1931)
Donovan, Vincent, *Christianity Rediscovered: An Epistle from the Maasai* (Maryknoll, NY: Orbis Books, 1982)
Doyle, Dennis M., *Communion Ecclesiology* (Maryknoll, NY: Orbis Books, 2000)
Dunne, John, *The Way of All the Earth: Experiments in Truth and Religion* (London: Macmillan, 1972)
Dupuis, J., *Toward a Christian Theology of Religious Pluralism* (Maryknoll, NY: Orbis Books, 1997)

Eagleton, Terry, *Hope Without Optimism* (New Haven, CT: Yale, 2015)
Eck, D. L., *A New Religious America* (New York: HarperOne, 2001)
Eco, Umberto, and Cardinal Martini, *Belief or Unbelief? A Confrontation* (New York: Arcade, 1997)
Eco, Umberto, *The Name of the Rose* (London: Vintage, 2004)
Eliot, T. S., *The Idea of a Christian Society* (London: Faber & Faber, 1939)
Eliot, T. S., *Christianity and Culture* (New York: Harvest Books, 1977)
Enayat, Hamid, *Modern Islamic Political Thought* (London: I.B. Tauris, 2005)
Esposito, John L., Fasching, Darrell, J. and Lewis, Todd, *Religion and Globalization: World Religions in Historical Perspective* (Oxford: Oxford University Press, 2008)
Every, George, *Poetry and Responsibility* (London: SCM, 1949)
Every, George, *Byzantine Patriarchate* (London: SPCK, 1962)
Every, George, *Christian Mythology* (London: Hamlyn, 1970)
Every, George, Harries, Richard and Ware, Kallistos, *Seasons of the Spirit* (London: SPCK, 1984)

Fenton, John, *St Matthew's Gospel* (London: Pelican, 1963)
Ferguson, Ron and Chater, Mark, *Mole Under the Fence: Conversations with Roland Walls* (Norwich: St Andrew Press, 2006)
Fermor, Patrick Leigh, *A Time to Keep Silence* (London: John Murray, 1957)
Figgis, J.N., *Churches in the Modern State* (London: Longmans, Green and Co. 1913)

Foley, Michael and Hoge, Dean, *Religion and the New Immigrants* (Oxford: Oxford University Press, 2007)

Habermas, Jurgen, *An Awareness of What is Missing: Faith and Reason in a Post Secular Age* (London: Polity Press, 2010)
Harnack, Adolf Von, *What is Christianity?* (London: E. Benn, 1901)
Harries, Richard, and Mayr-Harting, Henry, eds, *Christianity Two Thousand Years* (Oxford: Oxford University Press, 2001)
Harries, Richard, *God Outside the Box* (London: SPCK, 2002)
Hebblethwaite, B., *Ethics and Religion in a Pluralistic Age* (Edinburgh:T. & T. Clark, 1997)
Hebert, Gabriel, *God's Kingdom and Ours* (London: SCM, 1959)
Hick, John, *Who or What is God?* (London: SCM, 2008)
Hillesum, Etty, *An Interrupted Life: The Diaries and Letters of Etty Hillesum 1941-1943* (London: Persephone Books, 1999)
Holloway, Richard, *Leaving Alexandria* (Edinburgh: Canongate, 2012)
Holloway, Richard, *A Little History of Religion* (New Haven, CT:Yale, 2016)
Hooker, Richard, *Of the Laws of Ecclesiastical Polity Vols 1 & 2* (Oxford: Oxford University Press, 1841)
Hopkins, Gerard Manley, Gardner, W.W., ed., *Poems and Prose* (Harmondsworth: Penguin, 1953)

Iqbal, M., *Science and Islam* (Westport, CT: Greenwood Press, 2007)

Johnston, William, *The Inner Eye of Love: Mysticism and Religion* (London: Collins, 1978)

Kandinsky, W., Sadler, Michael, T.H., trans., *Concerning the Spiritual in Art* (London:Tate, 2006)
Kearney, Richard, *Anatheism: Returning to God After God* (New York, NY: Columbia University Press, 2011)
Kelly, Herbert, *An Idea in the Working: An Account of the Society of the Sacred Mission, its History and Aims* (London: Mowbray, 1908)
Kelly, Herbert, *The Gospel of God* (London: SCM, 1959)
Kermode, Frank, *The Sense of an Ending* (Oxford: Oxford University Press, 2000)
Khalidi, T., *The Muslim Jesus* (Cambridge, MA: Harvard University Press, 2003)
Kung, Hans and Moltmann, Jurgen, eds, *Fundamentalism as Ecumenical Challenge: Concilium Special* (London: SCM, 1992)

Lapsley, Michael, *Redeeming the Past* (Maryknoll, NY: Orbis Books, 2012)
Lewis, B., *Cultures in Conflict* (Oxford: Oxford University Press, 1995)
Lewis, C. S., *Weight of Glory* (London: HarperCollins, 2001)
Lindbeck, George, *The Nature of Doctrine, Religion and Theology in a Post Liberal Age* (London:Westminster Press, 1994)
Linzey, Andrew and Kirker, Richard, eds, *Gays and the Future of Anglicanism* (Ropley, Hants: O Books, 2005)

SELECT BIBLIOGRAPHY

Living with Difference: Community, Diversity and the Common Good, Report of the Commission on Religion and Belief in British Public Life (Cambridge: The Woolf Institute, 2015)

Loisy, Alfred, *La Naissance du Christianism* (London: Allen & Unwin, 1948)

Loisy, Alfred, *Gospel and the Church* (Amherst, NY: Prometheus, 1988)

McManners, John, ed., *The Oxford Illustrated History of Christianity* (Oxford: Oxford University Press, 2001)

MacCulloch, Diarmaid, *Silence in the History of the Church* (Harmondsworth: Penguin, 2011)

MacCulloch, Diarmaid, *All Things made New* (London: Allen Lane, 2016)

Macquarrie, John, *On Being a Theologian* (London: SCM, 1999)

Maitland, Donald, *Diverse Times, Sundry Places* (London: Alpha Press, 1996)

Mannion, Gerald, *Ecclesiology and Post Modernity: Questions for the Church in our Time* (Collegeville, MN: Liturgical Press, 2007)

Markus, Robert, *The End of Ancient Christianity* (Cambridge: Cambridge University Press, 1990)

March, R. and Tambimuttu, *T.S Eliot: A Symposium* (New York, NY: Tambimuttu & Mass, 1948)

Martin, Ralph, *Towards a New Day* (London: Darton, Longman and Todd, 2015)

Merton, Thomas, *Conjectures of a Guilty Bystander* (Harmondsworth: Penguin, 1968)

Miles, Sara, *Jesus Freak* (San Francisco, CA: Jossey-Bass, 2010)

Miller, Charles, *Richard Hooker and the Vision of God* (Cambridge: James Clarke & Co., 2013)

Miller, John, *A Simple Life: Roland Walls and the Community of the Transfiguration* (Norwich: St Andrew Press, 2014)

Morgan, Teresa, *Roman Faith and Christian Faith* (Oxford: Oxford University Press, 2016)

Morley, Georgina, *John Macquarrie's Natural Theology: The Grace of Being* (Farnham, Surrey: Ashgate, 2003)

Moses, John, *Divine Discontent: The Prophetic Voice of Thomas Merton* (London: Bloomsbury, 2014)

Mostyn, T., *Censorship in Islamic Societies* (London: Saqi Books, 2002)

Nasr, Seyyed Hossein, *Religion and the Order of Nature* (Oxford: Oxford University Press, 1996)

Nicholls, David, *The Pluralist State* (London: Macmillan, 1994)

Nineham, Dennis, *Saint Mark* (London: Westminster Press, 1963)

Nineham, Dennis, *The Use and Abuse of the Bible: A Study of the Bible in an Age of Rapid Change* (London: Macmillan, 1976)

Ogilvie, Sarah, *Words of the World: A Global History of the Oxford English Dictionary* (Cambridge: Cambridge University Press, 2013)

Origo, Iris, *The Merchant of Prato: Francesco di Marto Datini 1335-1410* (Boston, MA: Nonpareil Books, 2002)

Pannenberg, W., *Christianity in a Secularised World* (London: SCM, 1998)
Peterson, Michael, Hasker, William, Reichenbach, Bruce and Basinger, David, *Reason and Religious Belief* (Oxford: Oxford University Press, 2003)

Rahner, Karl, *Foundations of the Christian Faith: An Introduction to the Idea of Christianity* (Chicago, IL: IPG, 1978)
Rashid, A., *Taliban: The Story of the Afghan Warlords* (London: Pan Macmillan, 2001)
Raison, Timothy and Marder, Lucy, ed., *We Three Kings: The Magi in Art and Legend* (Aylesbury: Hazell Books, 1995)
Rand, Ayn and Brandon, Nathaniel, *The Virtue of Selfishness* (New York, NY: Signet, 1964)
Robinson, Edward, ed., *Living the Questions* (Studies in Religious Experience) (Oxford: Oxford University Press, 1978)
Rovelli, Carlo, Carnell, Simon and Segre, Erica, trans., *Seven Brief Lessons on Physics* (London: Allen Lane, 2015)
Rouner, Leroy, ed., *Civil Religion and Political Theology* (Notre Dame, IN: University of Notre Dame, 1980)
Russell, Anthony, *The Clerical Profession* (London: SPCK, 1980)
Russell, Norman, *Fellow Workers with God: Orthodox Thinking on Theosis* (New York: St Vladimir's Seminary Press, 2009)
Russello, Gerald J., ed., *Christianity and European Culture: Selections from the work of Christopher Dawson* (Baltimore, MD: Catholic University Press of America, 1998)

Sacks, J., *The Persistence of Faith* (Reith Lectures, 1990)
Sagovsky, N. and McGrail, P., eds, *Together for the Common Good* (London: SCM, 2015)
Shaw, Jane and Kreider, Alan, *Culture and the Non-conformist Tradition* (Cardiff: University of Wales Press, 1999)
Shortt, Rupert, *God is No Thing: Coherent Christianity* (London: C. Hurst and Co., 2016)
Siddiqui, Mona, *Hospitality and Islam* (New Haven, CT: Yale, 2015)
Soroush, A., *Reason, Freedom and Democracy in Islam* (Oxford: Oxford University Press, 2000)
Soskice, Janet Martin, *Sisters of Sinai: How two Lady Adventurers Found the Hidden Gospels* (New York: Chatto & Windus, 2009)
Spong, John Shelby, *Why Christianity Must Change or Die* (London: HarperCollins, 1999)
Strudwick, Vincent, 'Harmonious Dissimilitude' in 'Gays and the Future of Anglicanism: Responses to the Windsor Report, Andrew Linzey and Richard Kirker eds. (Winchester and New York: John Hunt Publishing, 2005)
Strudwick, Vincent, 'C S Lewis in context: Christian apologetic between the wars and after', in 'The Chronicle of the Oxford University C S Lewis Society, Vol. 3 Issue 3 October 2006.

Tawney, R. H., *Religion and the Rise of Capitalism* (Kowloon, Hong Kong: Hesperides Press, 2006)

Taylor, John V., *A Christmas Sequence and Other Poems* (Oxford: Amate Press, 1989)

Taylor, John V., *The Go-Between God* (London: SCM, 2010)

Taylor, John V., *The Primal Vision* (London: SCM, 2010)

Temple, William, *Personal Religion and the Life of Fellowship* (London: Longmans, Green and Co., 1926)

Temple, William, *Christian Faith and Life* (London: SCM, 1931)

Temple, William, *Nature, Man and God* (London: Macmillan, 1934)

Temple, William, *Readings in St John's Gospel: First Series, Chapters 1-X11* (London: Macmillan, 1939)

Temple, William, *The Hope of a New World* (London: Macmillan, 1947)

Temple, William and Preston, Ronald, ed., *Christianity and Social Order* (London: SPCK, 1976)

Titmus, Colin, ed., *Lifelong Education for Adults: An International Handbook* (Oxford: Pergamon Press, 1989)

Towards a Quaker View of Sex: An Essay by a Group of Friends (Friends Home Service Committee New Edn, 1964)

Trigg, Roger, *Religion in Public Life: Must Faith be Privatised?* (Oxford: Oxford University Press, 2007)

Vermes, Geza, *Jesus the Jew* (Minneapolis, MN: Augsburg Fortress, 2003)

Vermes, Geza, *Christian Beginnings: From Nazareth to Nicaea* (New Haven, CT: Yale, 2012)

Vermes, Geza, *The Resurrection* (London: Penguin, 2008)

Ward, Keith, *A Vision to Pursue* (London: SCM, 1991)

Ward, Keith, *Is Religion Irrational?* (Oxford: Lion Books, 2011)

Williams, Rowan, *Lost Icons* (Edinburgh: T. & T. Clarke, 2000)

Williams, Rowan, *Anglican Identities* (London: Darton, Longman and Todd, 2004)

Williams, Rowan, *Christian Imagination in Poetry and Polity* (Oxford: SLG Press, 2004)

Williams, Rowan, *Grace and Necessity* (London: Continuum, 2005)

Williams, Rowan, *Why Study the Past? The Quest for the Historical Church* (London: Darton, Longman and Todd, 2005)

Williams, Rowan, *A Silent Action* (London: SPCK, 2013)

Williams, Rowan, *The Edge of Words* (London: Bloomsbury, 2014)

Wilson, A.N., *Against Religion* (London: Chatto & Windus, 1991)

Wilson, A.N., *God's Funeral* (London: John Murray, 1999)

Wilson, Colin, *The Outsider* (London: Gollancz, 1956)

The Windsor Report (London: Morehouse, 2004)

Wright, N.T., Ward, Keith and Hebblethwaite, Brian, *The Changing Face of God: Lincoln Lectures in Theology 1996* (Lincoln: Lincoln Cathedral Publications, 1996)

Zizioulas, John, *Being as Communion: Studies in Personhood and the Church* (London: Darton, Longman and Todd, 1985)

Index

INDEX